THAILAND
POLITICS, ECONOMY, AND SOCIO-CULTURAL SETTING

THAILAND
POLITICS, ECONOMY, AND SOCIO-CULTURAL SETTING

A SELECTIVE GUIDE TO THE LITERATURE

Woodworth G. Thrombley
William J. Siffin

Indiana University Press / Bloomington & London
for the International Affairs Center

Copyright © 1972 by Indiana University Press

ALL RIGHTS RESERVED

No part of this book may be reproduced or utilized in any form or by any means, electronic or mechanical, including photocopying and recording, or by any information storage and retrieval system, without permission in writing from the publisher. The Association of American University Presses Resolution on Permissions constitutes the only exception to this prohibition.

Published in Canada by Fitzhenry & Whiteside Limited, Don Mills, Ontario

Library of Congress catalog card number: 75-126218 | ISNB: 253-35850-7
Manufactured in the United States of America

TO LAURISTON SHARP

whose contribution is manifest in the
finest applications of the social sciences
to the contemporary study of Thailand

ACKNOWLEDGMENTS

The compilation of this bibliographic guide — an on-again, off-again effort over about seven years — owes a great deal to a number of people. Many of the items were first collected in Bangkok and appeared in a prefatory Thai and English-language bibliography published by the National Institute of Development Administration in 1967 for circulation in Thailand: *The Thai Government and its Setting: A Selective Annotated Bibliography*. We are grateful to our colleagues at NIDA for their help in that effort, especially to Professors Pensri Vayavananda, Choop Karnjanaprakorn, and Amara Raksastaya. We are also grateful to Mrs. Barbara Schaaf, chief secretary of the MUCIA advisory group at NIDA, and to Professor Peter Bell, now at the University of British Columbia, for their contributions to that earlier volume.

We wish to thank also Professor M. Ladd Thomas, Director of the Center for Southeast Asian Studies at Northern Illinois University, and Lee Dutton, Southeast Asian Librarian at Northern Illinois, for their generous counsel and help in making Thai materials at NIU available to us for the work at hand. Our thanks go, too, to Dr. Toshio Yatsushiro, former advisor to the Thai Department of Community Development, and to Khun Somporn Sangchai, a staff member of the AID-Bangkok research division, for their helpful suggestions and for copies of research publications; to Professor Charles F. Keyes, Department of Anthropology, University of Washington, for his review of and contribution to the section on Socio-Cultural Characteristics of Contemporary Thailand; to Professor W. David Maxwell of the Indiana University Business School for his review of and contribution to the section on the Thai Economy and Economic Development; to Miss Joyce Smith, a doctoral candidate in the Department of Political Science at Indiana University, who assisted in the collection of materials; and to Professor Lauriston Sharp, who generously permitted us to make use of material from the Cornell Bibliography.

The editorial assistance of Mrs. Martha Wailes is gratefully acknowledged, along with the valuable advice of Mrs. Edith G.

Albee and Mrs. Pamela Scheinman of the International Affairs Center Publications at Indiana University Press. The typing was done by Mrs. Kay Long, Mrs. Joan Singer, and Miss Karen Tkach, for whose patient forbearance we can only rejoice.

We also wish to acknowledge the financial assistance of Indiana University's International Development Research Center which has helped make publication possible.

W.G.T.
W.J.S.

CONTENTS

Foreword by Lynne L. Merritt, Jr.   *xi*

Introduction   *xiii*

A Note on the Literature About Thailand   *xv*

A. GENERAL REFERENCE MATERIALS	1
B. THE HISTORICAL BACKGROUND OF CONTEMPORARY THAILAND	12
1. General Historical Background	13
2. Thailand and the West	19
C. CONTEMPORARY POLITICS	23
1. Political Leaders and the Political System	25
2. Interests and Associations	30
3. Law, Justice, and the Courts	31
4. The Military, National Security, and Communism	32
5. Subnational Government	35
6. Contemporary Diplomacy and International Relations	44
D. THE BUREAUCRACY AND PUBLIC ADMINISTRATION	49
1. The Administrative System	50
2. Personnel and Civil Service	55
3. Revenue and Finance Administration	56
E. THE THAI ECONOMY AND ECONOMIC DEVELOPMENT	58
1. The Economy	59

2. Foreign Trade	69
3. Planning and Economic Development	72
4. Statistical Sources	79
F. EDUCATION	83
1. Higher Education	84
2. Elementary and Secondary Education	87
G. SOCIO-CULTURAL CHARACTERISTICS OF CONTEMPORARY THAILAND	91
1. The Social Structure and Social Change	91
2. Religion	104
3. Art, Language, Literature, and Drama	108
4. Minorities: Chinese, Muslims, Thai-Lao, and Hill Tribes	114
5. Population	120
H. BIBLIOGRAPHIES AND RELATED ITEMS	122
I. OTHER SOURCES OF INFORMATION	131
1. Academic Programs	131
2. Organizations and Other Data Sources	133
3. Directories	137
4. Major Journals	139
5. English-Language Newspapers and Periodicals	140
6. Booksellers	141
Index	143

FOREWORD

This bibliographic guide is one product of a venture in cooperation that began over fourteen years ago with agreements between Indiana University, the Thai College of Education, Thammasat University, and the Agency for International Development. Today the effort continues in new and expanded form, with Indiana University and the four other members of the Midwest Universities Consortium for International Affairs, aided by the Ford Foundation, all joined to assist the Thai National Institute of Development Administration in its formative years.

Some of the fruits of Indiana University's association are reflected in the contents of this work — books and articles by members of our faculty, and the numerous theses, dissertations and other useful studies by Thais who have been the chief participants in our joint enterprises. The Thai studies produced by our faculty, past and present, have been greatly aided by the access to materials and assistance that has been generously provided by our Thai associates. We, in turn, are pleased to have played a supporting role in the growing contribution of Thais to the study of Thai government and its setting.

This work is the result of cooperative academic efforts. Professors Thrombley and Siffin share primary responsibility, but much assistance, acknowledged elsewhere, was received from the staff of the Thai Institute of Public Administration and its successor organization, the National Institute of Development Administration.

As I look back over the record of Indiana University's cooperative associations with Thailand, I regard this bibliographic guide with particular satisfaction. It is in itself a useful scholarly tool, and it also documents the swelling stream of scholarship in this area, a literature to which we at the University are pleased to have added a small share. The further aim of international cooperation must always be to add to the store of our knowledge and to expand the range of mankind's capabilities. This little volume, and some of the citations it contains, are evidence that one particular venture in cooperation has achieved gratifying results.

Lynne L. Merritt, Jr.
Vice President and Dean,
Research and Advanced Studies

Indiana University
December, 1970

INTRODUCTION

About a hundred years ago, some long-forgotten commentator on the Thai scene wrote down this prediction: of all the countries of Asia including Japan, Thailand — or as it was then called, Siam — showed the greatest potential for modernization; Siam would enter the twentieth century an urban, industrial nation. History took little note of the man who made this forecast, but the evidence of his error has been writ large. Thailand continued for a long time without any stark discontinuity in its culture and its social structure. In many ways, persistence and stability have been dominant themes in the nation's history, until quite recently. Today the cumulative effects of accelerating development become ever more apparent. Thailand changes at a growing rate, with an expanding impact.

This change is reflected in the literature available for the study of Thailand. That literature proliferates. Today's scholar is confronted with a profusion of materials, and still more are forthcoming. Therefore, we have prepared this selective bibliographical guide to offer a baseline for the scholar interested in studying Thai government and its social, economic, and cultural context. If we have done our job adequately, the scholar can wrestle with the problem of sources, knowing that a basic collection of the good (and some that he may find not so good) English-language materials produced through 1969 has been identified and briefly described.

We have also sought to identify key sources of future information. Any bibliography is out of date by the time it is published, or even before. There is probably more material about Thailand in the making at this moment than has been produced in the past twenty years. Much of this future material will flow to comparatively few centers; most of it will be recorded in a relatively small number of sources; and a good bit will be produced at places that can be identified. We do not claim to have identified all the places to look for Thai materials in the 1970's, but we have indicated the sources that are most likely to prove rewarding. Nor have we tried to duplicate existing general bibliographies, which are themselves cited and supplemented here.

Most of the materials cited are of recent origin, although a fairly large number of older items of particular value are also included. Practically all of the cited literature is in English. Selected dissertations, theses, and unpublished papers also are cited since access is often available to such materials, and some of them contain data otherwise difficult to acquire.

An attempt has been made to incorporate materials reflecting the perspectives, concepts, and methods of contemporary social sciences, in addition to other items which, although they are simple descriptions or subjective interpretations, are of particular use to social scientists. We have sought to classify and briefly describe items in a way that will enable the prospective reader of this bibliography to make a preliminary judgment of their usefulness to him.

A NOTE ON THE LITERATURE ABOUT THAILAND

The history of Siam, on one hand, merges into archaeology and, on another, blurs into fable. In the manner of Oriental kingdoms, chronicles that were made and kept at the royal palace recorded important events in Siamese history over more than five hundred years. From these, and from inscriptions, records of edicts, and the chronicles of other nations such as Burmese kingdoms and China, an outline of ancient Siamese history has been reconstructed by both Thai and Western scholars. Notable among these historical sources are portions of D. G. E. Hall's *History of Southeast Asia* and the work of W. A. R. Wood, one-time British Consul General at Chiengmai, whose outline of old Thai history exemplifies the contribution made by a number of foreign officials to our knowledge of Thailand. The scholarship of other Westerners who came to Thailand to participate in its modernization during the late nineteenth and early twentieth centuries is an important source of background data on contemporary Thailand, and much of it can be found in issues of the *Journal of the Siam Society*, published annually in Bangkok since 1904, except during World War II. The development of Thai scholarship in history and related areas can also be sketched, to some extent, by reference to the *Journal*.

As for ancient Thai sources, many were lost in the sack of the Siamese capital, Ayudhya, by the Burmese in 1767. But one of the major aims of the first king of the Chakri dynasty (or Bangkok era) was to recollect and record the laws, rituals, and traditions of the past. The annals of the Ayudhyan dynasty (1350-1767) were reconstructed and eventually published in 1912. These *Pharatchaponsawadan chabap praratchahatleka* are a useful source of insight into the nature and concerns of ancient Thai royalty. Later the annals of the first five kings of the Chakri dynasty were also published. They are among the pertinent records of the nineteenth-century Thai government.

xvi   Thailand: Politics, Economy, and Socio-Cultural Setting

Studies of Thailand and its government by Westerners began to appear in growing numbers a little more than a hundred years ago, with the coming of American Protestant missionaries and Western traders, diplomats, governmental aides, and advisors. A few others trace back to the seventeenth century and earlier, to such materials as the description of Siam by Simon de la Loubère, published in Paris in 1691 and in London two years later.

In 1688 Siam withdrew from contact with the West. By the nineteenth century, however, with the British in Burma and the French in Indochina, Western nations could no longer be ignored. For the past century and a half, the history of Thailand has comprised a series of accommodations to Western politics, economics, technology, and culture. Much of this history has been written by Westerners, figuratively through their contributions to the modernization of the country, and literally through accounts of their efforts and experiences and their studies in fields ranging from archaeology to anthropology. George Coedès, Robert Lingat, H. G. Quaritch Wales, August Pavie, Reginald le May, Erik Seidenfaden, O. Frankfurter, G. E. Gerini, and Walter Graham are among the notable names in the literature concerning Thailand that emerged during and after the astounding epoch known as the Chakri Reformation — the governmental modernization begun by King Mongkut (1854-1867) and carried forward by his distinguished son, King Chulalongkorn (1867-1910).

This reformation also produced Thai writings important to the study of the nation and its government, among them the correspondence, messages, and edicts of that legendary potentate, Mongkut. In the reign of his son, reports and statistics began to appear, along with a mounting flow of laws and regulations in the Western style. At the same time, a new Thai scholarship was exemplified and nurtured by one of the most impressive men in Thailand's long history: Prince Damrong Rajanubhab, Minister of Interior, renovator of the National Library, promoter of modern education in Thailand, and no mean scholar in his own right.

Damrong's followers have been few in number. Less than ten per cent of the citations in the Thai section of John Embree and Lillian Dotson's *Bibliography of the Peoples and Culture of Mainland Southeast Asia* refer to Thai authors. Prince Damrong had a respect bordering on reverence for his nation's heritage, and he devoted time, effort, and expense to the collection of artifacts as well as documents of value to future scholars. But the forces of history conspired to thwart many of the hopes he may have had concerning Thai scholarship. The reconstruction of the government claimed most of the available talent. The institutions of higher education which emerged in the twentieth century were committed to teaching and training rather than to research. And intellectual efforts have had to be largely self-rewarding and self-financed in the particular context of Thai society. For these and other reasons, scholarship in the humanities and the social sciences did not flourish among Thais, although the situation is now changing.

Well into this century much of the writing about Thailand and its government was descriptive, and to a considerable extent, subjective. The most systematic work concerned history, archaeology, anthropology, and the natural sciences. As for assessments of the Thai people and their governmental and economic arrangements, one finds rather sweeping personal judgments recorded as early as 1870 by Mrs. Anna Leonowens, tutor to the children of King Mongkut, and as recently as 1941 by Virginia Thompson, in her book *Thailand, the New Siam*.

Studies consciously reflecting the perspectives, concepts, and methods of the modern social sciences began to appear in the 1930's. One of the first was Professor Carl C. Zimmerman's systematic survey of the economic characteristics of rural Thailand, published in 1931. Other works of this new era included Kenneth Perry Landon's study of the cultural trends in post-revolutionary Thailand, covering the five years following the 1932 revolution. During the 1930's, Reginald le May was engaged in research for his *Culture of Southeast Asia*, published in 1954, and Erik Seidenfaden was pursuing the anthropological and ethnological work that culminated in a monograph, *The Thai Peoples* (1958), not published until after his death. H. G. Quaritch Wales, who approached the study of Siamese court ceremonies from a semi-sociological perspective, Robert Lingat, systematically studying Siamese law as well as religion, and George Coedès, examining and evaluating information on Thai culture and history, were among the Westerners in the 1930's engaged in studies that might be classed within the social sciences.

But the literature of Thai economics, politics, sociology, and social anthropology did not really flourish until the years following World War II. The Southeast Asia Program of Cornell University was a prime source of impetus to work ranging from an examination of myriad aspects of existence in the village of Bang Chan to David Wilson's portrait of Thai national politics. Scholars from other Western universities have also made systematic contributions to an understanding of Thai government and society, as the following citations indicate. The post-war period has also been marked by a significant growth in the number of theses and dissertations concerned with Thai politics, economics, and sociocultural setting. These furnish a rough but relevant index of contemporary Western patterns of scholarship related to Thailand, and they are sometimes a fruitful source of information.

To mid-1968, 136 doctoral dissertations concerning Thailand were accepted at American universities.* Only five of them were completed before 1941; all but eleven were completed after 1950. Of the dissertations, eighty-eight were written by Thais, but forty-one of these were concerned with Thai education. Twenty-two of the dissertations written by Thai students were concerned with the Thai economy, sixteen with Thai international relations, government, politics and administration, and only one with aspects of Thai culture. Of the dissertations on Thai subjects not written by Thais, at least eighteen dealt with aspects of Thai culture and society, about thirteen were studies of facets of Thai international relations or domestic government, and the rest were distributed among economics, linguistics, history, and education.

The fact that nearly half of the dissertations written by Thais on Thai subjects were in the field of education is not surprising.** That twenty-three dealt with economics is again consistent with expectations. Of all the social sciences, the one best established in Thailand is economics. Thailand has an abiding commitment to economic development — a commitment linked with concern for national survival. The utility of economics has been demonstrated and accepted in the decision-making center of Thai government; the importance of sound fiscal and monetary policy has been recognized since early in the Chakri Reformation.

Six of the sixteen Thai dissertations that might roughly be classified as "political science" are concerned with international relations. This, too, is to be expected, in view of the importance of diplomacy to the only nation in Southeast Asia that escaped colonial domination by the West. The other dissertations in the field largely describe formal institutional aspects of Thai gov-

---

*The data that follow are from Lian The and Paul W. van der Veur, *Treasures and Trivia: Doctoral Dissertations on Southeast Asia Accepted by Universities in the United States* (Athens, Ohio: Center for International Studies, Ohio University, 1968), pages 125ff.

**The heavy concentration in education has been, in some part, a consequence of the availability of U.S. Agency for International Development and other foreign scholarship opportunities, i.e., influenced if not largely determined by foreign assistance grantors.

ernment; for example, one is a detailed description of the actors and events of the bloodless revolution of 1932, in which the Chakri dynasty was overthrown. The analysis of contemporary political processes in Thailand has not been the subject of dissertations by Thai scholars up to now. Nor had more than two Thai doctoral studies in the field of sociology been completed by mid-1968.

This survey of dissertations is not conclusive evidence of the disciplinary identification of Thai social scientists, since other Thais have written dissertations on non-Thai subjects. But the pattern found here is more or less suggestive of the position of the social sciences in Thailand, and of the kinds of social science perspectives and methods which have been brought to bear upon the study of Thailand by Thais.

One may summarize the state of the systematic literature concerning Thai government and its setting in terms of these characteristics:

First, to date most of it has been produced by non-Thais.

Second, only a small part of the relatively recent work has consisted of systematic analysis using the perspectives and methods of the social sciences — and most of this is in economics.

Third, little of this literature is currently available in the Thai language, although an increasing share of the findings in studies about Thailand has become available to Thai students through the lectures and textual materials of Thai instructors trained abroad in the social sciences.

Fourth, the literature on the Thai political system and its socio-cultural setting is quite uneven. Economics and education seem to be the most extensively covered subjects.

It is difficult to anticipate future developments in scholarship in the social sciences dealing with Thailand. The growth of a literature is not an end, but the derivative result of a large number of interacting aims and efforts.

The volume of systematic studies of Thai government and society will expand in the coming years. Large and rapid changes have been taking place in the advanced education of Thais. The number of Thai social scientists grows, and the foundations of Thai scholarship are expanding. Thai society is also growing in size and complexity at an almost explosive rate. Accordingly, the needs are increasing for studies by social scientists concerning what is happening. Furthermore, social sciences, with their utility as policy-making tools, can enhance the quality of decision-making in Thai government and business, and Thais have never been unwilling to adopt science and technology when their value is apparent. The continuing development of the Thai educational system also creates expanding needs and opportunities for social science studies in Thailand, and of Thailand. Finally, the continuing and growing involvement of Thais in an international community of scholars within the social sciences inevitably will promote the systematic study, by Thais as well as foreigners, of aspects of Thai government and society. On the other hand, much Thai work in the social sciences no doubt will appear in the form of technical reports and memoranda. Many of these items will probably never enter the universe of "literature."

The instrumentalities of scholarly communication and the incentives to engage in it must be developed if social science scholarship in Thailand is to grow. The National Institute of Development Administration's journal may be one promising means by which Thai scholars can reach Thai and, to some extent, international audiences. But this *Journal of Development Administration* is limited in scope and orientation, and has not been well-supported. Recently another journal has been established, by the Social Science Association of Thailand, published in Thai but with occasional English articles. The Social Science Association is itself a portent of scholarly development. By 1965 it had published twelve books, most of them texts, but at least one, cited below, an English-language study by a French economist.

The limited "size of the market" is not conducive to scholarly writing by Thais, in Thai, in the social sciences. Other limitations are probably more important, however, and these include the reward system for Thai educators. Up to this point, enhanced status and income have not been linked particularly to scholarly endeavors.

As for foreign scholarship, one problem is the exquisite difficulty of the Thai language. Nevertheless, American Peace Corps volunteers who have acquired both basic language competence and Thai field experience offer promise for the future. Out of this growing group is likely to come a number of scholars committed to applying the perspectives, concepts, and methods of the social sciences to the study of Thai government and society.

In short, the present state of literature in the area covered by this bibliographic guide leaves something to be desired by the scholar who would study Thai government and society from published sources. But there are interesting prospects, and the chances are that any future revision of this limited guide would incorporate a new group of penetrating studies. In fact, this publication is based on the assumption that now is a good time for a systematic but selective survey of the existing body of material. Soon the corpus will be too large to manage in this fashion. And hopefully, this effort may serve as a point of departure for future scholars confronted with an ever-growing mass of materials. If it can serve them as a base, by selectively identifying highly relevant items that have appeared as late as 1969, and by identifying key sources of information for the years ahead, then this work will have served its purpose.

W.J.S.
W.G.T.

THAILAND
POLITICS, ECONOMY, AND SOCIO-CULTURAL SETTING

A.
GENERAL REFERENCE MATERIALS

This section contains a few standard historical works and supplementary volumes, of which D. G. E. Hall, *A History of Southeast Asia,* John F. Cady, *Southeast Asia: Its Historical Development,* and George Coedès, *The Indianized States of Southeast Asia,* are the outstanding examples. Geographical source materials, most notably Charles A. Fisher's *Southeast Asia: A Social, Economic and Political Geography,* are also cited. Certain political, economic, ethnographic, and cultural studies which treat Thailand as part of the Southeast Asian region are likewise included here. Of particular interest is the oft-cited little volume *Social Forces in Southeast Asia* by Cora DuBois. Finally, two additional types of works are included: the handbooks which are broadly useful Thai reference sources, and a few of the popular and impressionistic volumes by experienced Western observers of the Thai scene. Of the latter, W. A. R. Wood's *Consul in Paradise* is a pleasant vignette. In his words, "It consists merely of a little of the froth collected by a cork which has floated for sixty-eight years on the seas of Siamese and Anglo-Siamese life."

Atlas of Physical, Economic and Social Resources of the Lower Mekong Basin. Washington, D.C.: Engineer Agency for Resources Inventories, Department of the Army, and the Tennessee Valley Authority, September, 1968. 257 pages.

This *Atlas* (prepared under the direction of the U.S. Agency for International Development by TVA and the Engineer Agency for Resources Inventories for the U.N. Committee for Coordination of Investigations of the Lower Mekong Basin) is an impressive inventory in cartographic and narrative form of natural and man-made resources within the drainage basin of the Mekong River. The inventory is classified into thirty-eight separate topics under three main section headings: physical resources, human resources, and social and economic infrastructure. The large collection of beautifully prepared, multicolored maps permits visual perception of various development possibilities and alternatives within the four riparian countries of the Lower Mekong Basin.

Benda, Harry J., and John A. Larkin (eds.). *The World of Southeast Asia: Selected Historical Readings.* New York: Harper & Row, 1967. 331 pages.

A collection of readings and documents, each prefaced by a brief author's statement, which focuses on the internal developments of various Southeast Asian societies rather than on their external relations. Emphasis is on the modern period, though a number of the selections are on pre-modern Southeast Asia. Many of the selections are by Asian authors and several deal specifically with Thailand.

Black, Eugene R. *Alternative in Southeast Asia.* New York: Praeger, 1969. 192 pages.

Argues that regionalism, focusing on the Mekong Basin, is the best alternative in Southeast Asia, and that the United States should work toward fostering this end, rather than acting in the role of "policeman" or withdrawing from the area. The foreword is by Lyndon B. Johnson.

Blanchard, Wendell, et al. *Thailand: Its People, Its Culture.* New Haven: Human Relations Area Files Press, 1958. 528 pages.

A useful general reference source on contemporary Thailand. This volume is dated in some respects and treats its materials somewhat unevenly, but contains detailed descriptions of everyday life, village organizations, religion, government, the arts, and social structure. Includes interpretations as well as facts.

Bone, Robert C. *Contemporary Southeast Asia.* New York: Random House, 1962. 132 pages.

A brief survey of the history, governments, politics, and social and cultural characteristics and problems of Southeast Asia, beginning with the era of Western colonization. Limited treatment of Thailand, but useful as a quick introductory survey of the region.

Burling, Robbins. *Hill Farms and Paddy Fields: Life in Mainland Southeast Asia.* Englewood Cliffs: Prentice-Hall, 1965. 180 pages.

An easy introduction, from an anthropological viewpoint, to aspects of Southeast Asia's traditional agricultural systems. Excludes Malaysia, Indonesia, and the Philippines.

Busch, Noel F. *Thailand: An Introduction to Modern Siam.* Princeton: Van Nostrand, 1959. 166 pages.

A sympathetic and readable popular introduction, with chapters on history, current affairs, government, religion, arts, customs, and people. Some perceptive personal observations.

Buss, Claude A. *The Arc of Crisis.* New York: Doubleday, 1961. 479 pages.

The "arc of crisis" extends from Japan to Pakistan, according to the author. The book is essentially an effort to explain the area in political and social terms, and to interpret Asian reactions to and perspectives on the United States and U.S. foreign policy values and objectives. Also discusses communism in the area. An informative essayistic work rather than a systematic analysis.

Butwell, Richard. *Southeast Asia Today – and Tomorrow: A Political Analysis.* Second revised edition. New York: Frederick A. Praeger, 1969. 245 pages.

A brief survey of government and politics in Southeast Asia which includes some treatment of Thailand.

Cady, John F. *Southeast Asia: Its Historical Development.* New York: McGraw-Hill, 1964. 657 pages.

An ambitious history, to the end of World War II, which covers much the same ground as Hall, although not always in comparable depth. Nevertheless this is a good historical introduction to Southeast Asia.

Cady, John F. *Thailand, Burma, Laos, and Cambodia.* Englewood Cliffs: Prentice-Hall, 1966. 152 pages.

A brief but informative monograph on the four Theravada Buddhist countries of Southeast Asia. Assumes that the cultural and historical development of the countries, derived in part from a common Indian heritage, can be correlated in a meaningful way. The emphasis is primarily pre-twentieth century.

Chu, Valentin. *Thailand Today: A Visit to Modern Siam.* New York: Thomas Y. Crowell, 1968. 200 pages.

A subjective account of personal experiences in Thailand, describing the socio-cultural changes taking place within that nation. Political and economic change are also treated briefly. Asserts that despite modernizing trends "Thailand's cultural borrowing will be selective and not destructive of the national psyche."

Coedès, George. *The Indianized States of Southeast Asia: An English Translation of Les États hindouisés d'Indochine et d'Indonésie.* Edited by Walter F. Vella and translated by Susan Brown Cowing. Honolulu: East-West Center Press, 1968. 403 pages.

 Perhaps no one has made a greater contribution to Southeast Asian classical scholarship than George Coedès. This book, first published in Hanoi in 1944 under the title *Histoire ancienne des états hindouisés d'Extrême-Orient,* is not so much a history as an attempt to offer a synthesis showing how the various elements of the history are related.

Coedès, George. *The Making of Southeast Asia.* Translated by H. M. Wright. Berkeley and Los Angeles: University of California Press, 1966. 268 pages.

 This survey, originally published in 1962 as *Les Peuples de la peninsula indochinoise: Histoire-civilisations,* traces the development of the mainland states from prehistoric times, through the Indianization of Burma, Thailand, Laos, and Cambodia and the Sinicization of Vietnam, to the decline of Indian influence in the thirteenth century.

Credner, Wilhelm. *Siam, Das Land Der Tai.* Stuttgart: J. Engelbhorns, 1936. 422 pages.

 A geography based upon extensive field study in the late 1920's. Includes data on geology, climate, rainfall, land and water resources, as well as on the people, the government, and the economy. A thorough and useful work, still in many ways the single most authoritative Western-language source of geographical information on Thailand.

Cressey, George B. *Asia's Lands and Peoples.* Second edition. New York: McGraw-Hill, 1963. 597 pages.

 A popular geography text that includes a chapter on Thailand. A brief bibliography (p. 567) identifies a few items not noted in this guide.

Crozier, Brian. *Southeast Asia in Turmoil.* London: Penguin, 1965. 206 pages.

 A British journalist's interpretation of communism and military conflict in the region. Some discussion of SEATO and American policy in Southeast Asia.

Dobby, E. H. G. *Monsoon Asia.* Chicago: Quadrangle Books, 1961. 380 pages.

 A standard geographical reference, containing a short chapter on the physical geography of continental Southeast Asia, and information on economic and political geography.

Döhring, Karl Siegfried. *Siam*. 2 vols. Munich: Georg Müller, 1923.

German-language descriptive treatment by an art historian and ethnographer who also wrote extensively on Thai art and religion.

DuBois, Cora. *Social Forces in Southeast Asia*. New edition. Cambridge: Harvard University Press, 1959. 78 pages.

Originally presented in the form of three lectures delivered at Smith College in 1947, these essays are interesting for their predictions concerning political and social development in Southeast Asia.

Embree, John F., and William L. Thomas, Jr. *Ethnic Map and Gazetteer of Northern Southeast Asia*. New Haven: Southeast Asian Studies, Yale University, 1950. 175 pages.

Ethnolinguistic data on people of Yunnan, North Burma, Laos, Vietnam, and Thailand.

Emerson, Rupert. *Representative Government in Southeast Asia*. Cambridge: Harvard University Press, 1955. 197 pages.

Includes a brief discussion of lawmaking institutions in Thailand as of the mid-1950's.

Exell, F. K. *The Land and People of Thailand*. London: Adam and Charles Black; New York: Macmillan, 1960. 96 pages.

A short popular sketch, broad in scope and sympathetic in treatment. Like the Busch volume mentioned above, this is a simple, discerning, and informative book.

Fifield, Russell H. *Southeast Asia in United States Policy*. New York: Frederick A. Praeger, 1963. 488 pages.

One of the best standard textbooks in the field. Examines the evolution of American policy in Southeast Asia, communism, SEATO, the Laotian crisis, and the regional influence of Japan and India.

Fisher, Charles Alfred. *Southeast Asia: A Social, Economic and Political Geography*. Second edition. London: Methuen, 1967. 831 pages.

This is the most comprehensive survey of contemporary Southeast Asia available — a scholarly textbook, erudite, and beautifully organized. The first six chapters deal with the region as a whole. The following fifteen chapters examine the countries individually, detailing their social, economic and political problems in the appropriate geographical setting. A final chapter considers the changing relationships of the region with the outside world.

Ginsburg, Norton. *The Pattern of Asia.* Englewood Cliffs: Prentice-Hall, 1958. 929 pages.

A standard work on geography, distinguished by the range of its coverage. Includes a chapter on the geography of Thailand as part of a larger section on Southeast Asia. Some details are inevitably dated in a book that was five years in the writing, but this hardly impairs its basic value. A splendid set of maps and illustrations is included.

Golay, Frank., Ralph Anspach, M. Ruth Pfanner, and Eliezer B. Ayal. *Underdevelopment and Economic Nationalism in Southeast Asia.* Ithaca: Cornell University Press, 1969. 528 pages.

A valuable survey of economic nationalism in post-war Southeast Asia (Philippines, Indonesia, Burma, Thailand, Malaya, South Vietnam, and Cambodia), stressing local variation in economic policies. Nine "country" chapters, with the last essay summarizing and comparing principal indigenous aspects.

Gordon, Bernard K. *Toward Disengagement in Asia: A Strategy for American Foreign Policy.* Englewood Cliffs, N.J.: Prentice-Hall, 1969. 186 pages.

A balanced attempt to answer two basic questions: How can the nations of Asia best promote their own development? And what is America's national interest and role in that undertaking? Genuine regional cooperation and organization is seen as the answer to the first question; American policy and material support, as the answer to the second. The author considers Southeast Asia a power vacuum threatened by China, although the opposite view is noted fairly. (This book is about Southeast and East Asia, and not about Asia as a whole.)

Graham, Walter A. *Siam.* 2 vols. London: Alexander Moring, 1924.

The best comprehensive survey of Thailand as of the early twentieth century. Originally written in 1912, expanded in the later editions, and still germane. Volume I includes chapters on geography, history, social organization, ethnic groups, education, language, and literature. Volume II deals with industry, commerce, communications, art, and religion. Well-indexed and well-informed. Generous in its interpretation of the reign of Chulalongkorn's immediate successor.

Hall, D. G. E. *A History of Southeast Asia.* New York: St. Martin's Press, 1955. 807 pages.

A monumental history and valuable reference work. Organized chronologically by period as follows: pre-European, early phase of European expansion, European territorial expansion, period of nationalism and challenge to European domination. A revised 1964 edition includes additional material on the Philippines and on ex-colonial developments within Southeast Asia since 1950.

Harrison, Brian. *South-East Asia: A Short History.* Second edition, London: Macmillan; New York: St. Martin's Press, 1963. 270 pages.

Not as compendious as the Hall or Cady histories, and significantly less informative about Thailand.

Heine-Geldern, Robert. *Conceptions of State and Kingship in Southeast Asia.* Ithaca: Cornell University, Southeast Asia Program, Data Paper No. 18, 1963. 14 pages.

A brief comparative statement which includes a description of the position of the monarchy in traditional Thailand.

Insor, D. *Thailand: A Political, Social, and Economic Analysis.* New York: Frederick A. Praeger, 1963. 186 pages.

A popular introduction, interesting, readable, and informative. Fairly extensive description of modern Thai politics and foreign policy. Despite the title, this is not a systematic analysis.

Jayanama, Direck, Klaus Wenk, and Max Biehl. *Thailand.* Hamburg: Das Institut für Asienkunde; Frankfurt and Berlin: Alfred Metzner Verlag, 1960. 122 pages.

Three papers, one a description of Thai religion, government, society, and foreign relations by Khun Direck; the others are concerned with Thai-German relations and the domestic economy of Thailand.

Kennedy, J. *Asian Nationalism in the Twentieth Century.* New York: St. Martin's Press, 1968. 244 pages.

Part I is a survey and analysis of the varied patterns of modern Asian nationalism, covering Japan, China, the Indian subcontinent, Southeast Asia, and Western Asia. Part II consists of selections from the speeches and writings of Asian leaders and the accounts of contemporary observers. A well-written if somewhat thin source.

Lach, Donald F. *Southeast Asia in the Eyes of Europe: The Sixteenth Century.* Chicago: University of Chicago Press, 1968. 130 pages.

A reprint of Part III, Chapter VII, Volume I of the author's very fine *Asia in the Making of Europe.* The account, though partial and incomplete, reveals the prominence of Chinese and Muslims in the life of the region, the importance of Malacca in its commerce, the high degree of political independence of the continental states, and the isolation and primitive condition of some of the insular areas.

le May, Reginald S. *A Concise History of Buddhist Art in Siam.* See Section G-3.

le May, Reginald S. *The Culture of South-East Asia.* See Section G-3.

MacDonald, Alexander. *Bangkok Editor.* New York: Macmillan, 1949. 229 pages.

This book by the founder of the English-language Bangkok *Post* gives a general background on journalism in Bangkok, including material on press censorship, personnel, and advertising. Comments on political developments in early post-war Thailand.

Mills, Lennox A. *Southeast Asia: Illusion and Reality in Politics and Economics.* Minneapolis: University of Minnesota Press, 1964. 365 pages.

An economic and political survey. Includes brief treatments of post-monarchical Thai government and politics, of Thailand's China policy, and of foreign aid and investment. Perhaps one tenth of this book deals with Thai topics.

Myint, Hla. "The Inward and Outward Looking Countries of Southeast Asia and the Economic Future of the Region." See Section E-1.

Pendleton, Robert L., with Robert C. Kingsbury, *et al. Thailand: An American Geographical Society Handbook.* New York: Duell, Sloan and Pearce, 1962. 321 pages.

A useful reference volume, containing information on subjects ranging from geography and geology to agriculture and forestry. Includes statistical charts and tables, although the reference materials are often dated. The descriptions of geography and resources are particularly useful.

Report of the Asian Population Conference and Selected Papers. Bangkok: Economic Commission for Asia and the Far East; New York: United Nations Secretariat, 1964. 207 pages.
   An invaluable collection of papers on the demographic situation in Asia. Papers on: population trends; implications for educational planning, urban development, housing, and health programs; growth and structure of national production; measures for increasing employment; national policies aimed at influencing internal migration and urbanization; promotion of population research and training; and structure of the labor force in Asian countries.

Schaaf, C. Hart, and Russell H. Fifield. *The Lower Mekong: Challenge to Cooperation in Southeast Asia.* Princeton: Van Nostrand, 1963. 136 pages.
   Describes the physical potentialities for the development of the Lower Mekong River, and considers — from a rather optimistic view — the political and diplomatic requirements for implementing a scheme demanding substantial cooperation between Thailand and neighboring states. Schaaf was Executive Agent of the United Nation's Mekong Project.

Shaplen, Robert. *Time Out of Hand: Revolution and Reaction in Southeast Asia.* New York: Harper & Row, 1969. 465 pages.
   A superior survey of the contemporary Southeast Asian political scene by an outstanding commentator. The chapter on Thailand examines insurgency problems in the Northeast and the South, and government counterinsurgency programs.

Steinberg, David Joel (ed.). *In Search of Southeast Asia: A Modern History.* New York: Praeger Publishers, 1970. 544 pages.
   A regional history, organized along thematic lines that impose more of a focus than do other histories upon the mass of materials comprising the recorded background of this complex region. Begins with a well-organized survey of the Eighteenth Century, traces and assesses the impact of the West and the emergence of the foundations for new Southeast Asian states. Examines Twentieth Century nationalism and social change in Thailand and seven other Southeast Asian states. A distinctive treatment, marked by its analytic orientation, and by the fact that it is to an impressive degree a synthesis of contributions by six scholars, including David K. Wyatt, the

primary author of the Thai materials. Includes an extensive bibliography.

Thailand Official Yearbook, 1968. Bangkok: Office of the Prime Minister, 1968. 728 pages.

A collection of official information on many facets of Thailand. Fifteen sections and an appendix deal with government, foreign affairs, defense, welfare, health, and justice, as well as the economy. Also data on education, religion, art, sports, population, and tourism. The sections vary considerably in quality and much of the data is unreliable. (The previous edition of the *Yearbook* was published in 1964.)

Thompson, Virginia, and Richard Adloff. "Thailand (Siam)," in *The State of Asia: A Contemporary Survey.* New York: Alfred A. Knopf, 1959, pp. 268-291.

A brief, general account of political and economic developments in Thailand in the years immediately following World War II.

Tilman, Robert O. (ed.). *Man, State, and Society in Contemporary Southeast Asia.* New York: Frederick A. Praeger, 1969. 520 pages.

About thirty specialists describe and assess social, political, and economic characteristics of the Southeast Asian region and nine of its countries, including Thailand. The most recent and most comprehensive collection of readings intended for college text use.

U.S. Army Area Handbook for Thailand. Prepared by the Foreign Area Studies Division, Special Operations Research Office, American University, Washington, D.C., 1963. 487 pages.

A broad compilation of secondary-source information on Thai culture and society, politics, economics, and formal characteristics of the Thai military.

Von der Mehden, Fred. *Religion and Nationalism in Southeast Asia.* Madison: University of Wisconsin Press, 1959. 250 pages.

A study of the interaction of religion and nationalism in Southeast Asia and an attempt to show the extent to which religion is used to promote nationalism. Covers the region with particular emphasis on Burma, Indonesia, and the Philippines.

Wales, H. G. Quaritch. *Ancient Southeast Asian Warfare.* London: Bernard Quaritch, 1952. 206 pages.

Includes interesting descriptions of war as a facet of traditional Thai society, and discusses in idealized terms the relationship between Buddhism and militarism in traditional Thailand.

Wales, H. G. Quaritch. *Years of Blindness*. New York: Thomas Y. Crowell, 1943. 332 pages.

This book is useful not as a general history of Western imperialism in Asia, which it professes to be, but as an interesting personal commentary on the Thai monarchy in the 1920's and on the 1932 Thai revolution.

Wood, W. A. R. *Consul in Paradise: Sixty-nine Years in Siam*. London: Souvenir Press, 1965. 175 pages.

A personal, anecdotal account that captures a bit of the flavor of Thai culture in "the old days."

Young, Kenneth T., Jr. *The Southeast Asia Crisis, Background Papers and Proceedings of the Eighth Hammarskjold Forum*. New York: Oceana Publications, for the Association of the Bar of the City of New York, 1966. 226 pages.

An assessment of United States involvement in Southeast Asia by the former president of the Asia Society and former U.S. Ambassador to Thailand. Includes discussions of Chinese power and prospects for regionalism.

B.
THE HISTORICAL BACKGROUND OF CONTEMPORARY THAILAND

This section is divided into two parts. The first includes a series of items which deal broadly with Thai history, with the traditional monarchy and the early years of the post-monarchical period, or with various characteristics of Thailand at a particular stage in the nation's history. The absolute monarchy of traditional Thailand was one of the most significant features of the entire society. A number of the materials cited in this section contribute to an understanding of the kingship, especially the works of Wales and Vella. The other sources supplement these more general works.

As for the individual monarchs, one, King Mongkut (Rama IV), has been the subject of a number of Western-language biographical studies. Unfortunately, an equivalent treatment of his distinguished royal son, King Chulalongkorn (Rama V) is not available. Concerning the last two absolute monarchs of the Chakri Dynasty, Kings Vajiravudh (Rama VI) and Prajadhipok (Rama VII), Walter Vella and D. G. E. Hall have summed their achievements and their characters.

The second part of this section is concerned with Thailand's relations with the West. Thailand's first encounter with the West occurred in the sixteenth century following the Portuguese descent upon Malacca. Emissaries of the Portuguese General Albuquerque were sent to Siam because it was the nominal suzerain of the Malay sultanate. Little came of this mission, however, and Siam charted its own course during the sixteenth century.

The ancient kingdom also had a brief encounter with the West in the seventeenth century. After this episode came to an end in 1688, Thai-Western relations waned until the nineteenth century. Some of the key facts of nineteenth and twentieth century Thai history concern the Thai accommodation of Western forces and influences. Vella is a primary authority on Western impact, along with Wyatt. Valuable material will also be found in Hall and Cady, in the writings of Western observers cited in the first part of this section and in Section A, and in Section C-6.

1. General Historical Background

Bowring, Sir John. *The Kingdom and People of Siam: With a Narrative of the Mission to that Country in 1855.* 2 vols. London: Parker, 1857. 482 pages, 446 pages.

    A ranging description by a good observer of Thai society in the middle nineteenth century.

Cady, John F. *Southeast Asia: Its Historical Development.* See Section A.

Carter, A. Cecil (ed.). *The Kingdom of Siam.* New York: Putnam, 1904. 280 pages.

    This volume, prepared for the Louisiana Purchase Exhibition at St. Louis, Missouri, is an official description of Thai government and its setting at the height of the modernization efforts during the reign of King Chulalongkorn (1868-1910).

Chakrabongse, Prince Chula. *Lords of Life: The Paternal Monarchy of Bangkok, 1782-1932.* New York: Taplinger, 1960. 352 pages.

    Offered as a historical treatment of the Chakri Dynasty, and particularly of the later kings, this book was written by a British-educated member of Thai royalty. It is essentially a romantic and adulatory interpretation, and a poor history. Some useful factual information, but little that is novel and significant.

Choisy, Abbé François Timoléon de. *Journal du voyage de Siam fait en 1685 à 1686.* Reissued, with an introductory essay by Maurice Garcon. Paris: Editions du Charter and van Buggenhout, 1928. 296 pages.

    An illustrated edition of the classic account of the Abbé's voyage.

Chomchai, Prachoom. *Chulalongkorn the Great.* Tokyo. Center for East Asian Cultural Studies, 1965. 167 pages.

    Largely a translation of material from Salao Rekaruchi and Udom Pramuanwidhya, *Piya Maharaj Chulalongkorn,* Odeon Store, Bangkok, 1961. This, in turn, is a popular account based upon Prince Damrong Rajanubhab, *Praraj Pongsawadarn Krung Ratanakosin Rajakarn Tee 5,* a chronicle of the reign of King Chulalongkorn. Includes descriptions of some social, economic, and governmental changes during the reign of Rama

V, and some information about the personal life of the king. Useful information on the Chakri reformation.

Coedès, George. *The Indianized States of Southeast Asia: An English Translation of Les États hindouisés d'Indochine et d'Indonésie.* See Section A.

Coedès, George. *The Making of Southeast Asia.* See Section A.

Crawfurd, John. *The Crawfurd Papers.* Bangkok: Vajiranana National Library, 1915. 285 pages.

A collection of the official records relating to the 1821 mission of Dr. Crawfurd, published in English at the order of the Vajiranana National Library.

Crawfurd, John. *Journal of an Embassy from the Governor-General of India to the Courts of Siam and Cochin-China.* London: Colburn, 1928.

An interesting report of the 1821 mission, with impressions of the court and kingdom of the time, as well as of trade prospects.

Crosby, Sir Josiah. *Siam: The Crossroads.* London: Hollis & Carter Ltd., 1945. 174 pages.

A well-informed survey of Thai culture, history, government, and diplomatic relations with Britain, France, Japan, and China. A good account of the overthrow of the absolute monarchy in 1932. The author writes from his own experience of nearly twenty-five years in Thailand with the British foreign service.

Damrong Rajanubhab, Prince. *Miscellaneous Articles Written for the Journal of the Siam Society by His Late Royal Highness, Prince Damrong.* Bangkok: The Siam Society, 1962. 124 pages and 33 plates.

Consists of articles on Thai history and temple art, with 33 plates of Buddhist images. Articles include: "The Foundation of Ayudhya," "Preface to O. A. Frankfurter's Translation of Events in Ayudhya," "The Story of Records of Siamese History," "Siamese History Prior to the Founding of Ayudhya," "The Golden Pavilion of Wat Sai," "Angkor from a Siamese Point of View," and "The Introduction of Western Culture in Siam."

Dhani Nivat, Prince. "The Old Siamese Conception of the Monarchy." *Journal of the Siam Society,* vol. 36, part 2, 1947.

An authoritative sketch of the place of the kingship in the

traditional society. Reprinted in *Fiftieth Anniversary Commemorative Publication* (Selected articles from the *Journal of the Siam Society*). Bangkok: The Siam Society, 1954, pp. 160-175.

Dhani Nivat, Prince. "The Reconstruction of Rama I of the Chakkri Dynasty." *Journal of the Siam Society,* August, 1955, pp. 21-47.

   A historical narrative by a distinguished Thai scholar, describing the legal, historical, ceremonial, and artistic writings attributed to Phra Yodfa, Rama I of the Chakkri Dynasty, who established Bangkok as the national capital. Reprinted in *Lophburi, Bangkok, Bhuket: Selected Articles from the Journal of the Siam Society, Volume IV,* pp. 238-265, cited below.

Early History and Ayudhya Period: Selected Articles from the Journal of the Siam Society, Volume III. Bangkok: The Siam Society, 1959. 315 pages.

   Articles on the Ayudhyan period (1350-1767) and pre-Ayudhyan history and tradition. Notes on early Thai commerce, and other subjects.

Graham, Walter A. *Siam.* See Section A.

Griswold, Alexander B. *King Mongkut of Siam.* New York: The Asia Society, 1961. 60 pages.

   An expansion of an article originally published in the *Journal of the Siam Society* in April, 1957, and reprinted in *Lophburi, Bangkok, Bhuket: Selected Articles from the Journal of the Siam Society, Volume IV,* cited below.

Hall, D. G. E. *A History of Southeast Asia.* See Section A.

Harrison, Brian. *South-East Asia: A Short History.* See Section A.

la Loubère, Simon de. *A New Historical Relation of the Kingdom of Siam.* English-language edition. London, 1693.

   An interesting source of information about Thai culture and society of the late seventeenth century, and of Western perspectives thereon, growing out of the voyage of M. de la Loubère in 1688 and 1689.

Landon, Kenneth Perry. "Siam," in Lennox Mills, *et al., The New World of Southeast Asia.* Minneapolis: University of Minnesota Press, 1949, pp. 246-272.

   A summary of events and trends in Thailand from 1932 to 1948 by a scholar, missionary, and diplomatic advisor.

16   Thailand: Politics, Economy, and Socio-Cultural Setting

Landon, Kenneth Perry. *Siam in Transition.* Shanghai: Kelly and Walsh, 1939. U.S. distribution by University of Chicago Press. 328 pages. (Pirated edition, entitled *Thailand in Transition.* Bangkok, circa 1947. 427 pages.)

    A survey of apparent themes of change in Thai culture and society in the years following the 1932 revolution.

le May, Reginald S. *The Coinage of Siam.* Bangkok: The Siam Society, 1932. Reissued in 1961. 134 pages and plates.

    This seems to be the only English-language history of the coinage of Thailand.

Lophburi, Bangkok, Bhuket: Selected Articles from the Journal of the Siam Society, Volume IV. Bangkok: The Siam Society, 1959. 304 pages.

    The title is imprecise. The volume contains a number of articles on various aspects of Thai history, including the monarchy, and including commentaries on some early accounts by Western visitors to Thailand. Particularly relevant items are cited at appropriate locations within this bibliography.

Moffat, Abbot Low. *Mongkut, the King of Siam.* Ithaca: Cornell University Press, 1961. 254 pages.

    A sensitive and enthusiastic treatment, which is also well-organized and well-written. Together, Griswold and Moffat set straight the absurd and romantic record written by the one-time governess at the court of Siam, Mrs. Anna Leonowens, and give Mongkut the treatment he deserves as a vital figure in Thai history.

Pallegoix, Jean Baptiste. *Description du royaume Thai ou Siam, comprenant la topographie, histoire naturelle, moeurs et coûtumes, legislation, commerce, industrie, langue, littérature, religion, Annales des Thais et précis historique de la mission.* 2 vols. Paris: 1854.

    Bishop Pallegoix's study is as useful as it was ambitious; it contains a wealth of data about the topics included in his title. An English translation by R. F. Martins was published in Shanghai by the Celestial Empire Office, 1877.

Promoj, M. R. Seni. "King Mongkut as a Legislator." *Journal of the Siam Society,* January, 1950, pp. 32-66.

    Describes the innovative efforts of King Mongkut, including both his edicts and the modifications he undertook in the organization of Thai government during his reign (1851-1868). Reprinted in *Lophburi, Bangkok, Bhuket; Selected Articles from* the *Journal of the Siam Society, Volume IV*. Bangkok. The Siam Society, 1959, pp. 203-237.

Rabibhadana, Akin. *The Organization of Thai Society in the Early Bangkok Period, 1782-1783*. Ithaca: Cornell University, Southeast Asia Program, Data Paper No. 74, 1969. 245 pages.

Examination of social change in pre-modern Thailand. Demonstrates the importance of labor control and imperfections therein. Excellent piece of work.

Relationship with Burma; Parts I and II: Selected Articles from the Journal of the Siam Society, Volumes V and VI. Bangkok: The Siam Society, 1959. 207 pages, 228 pages.

Accounts of sixteenth, seventeenth, and eighteenth-century relations between Burma and Siam, drawn from *Hmannan Yazawin Dawgyi*, a history of Burma, compiled at the behest of King Bagyidaw of Burma in 1829. Also included is a chronicle of Thai history from Burmese sources for the period 1569-1767, known as "The Statement of Khun Luang Ha Wat." This is more fantastic than empirical, but interesting as a reflection of the spirit of its time and place.

Sarasas Bholakarn, Phra. *My Country Thailand (Its History, Geography and Civilization)*. Fifth Edition. Bangkok: 1956. 192 pages.

About three-fourths of this book is a history organized around the reigns of the sequence of Thai kings. Interesting because it reflects the perspective and assessments of a Thai author.

Siam: General and Medical Features. Bangkok: The Executive committee, Eighth Congress, Far Eastern Association of Tropical Medicine, 1930. 332 pages.

Twenty-five chapters by various advisors and officials in the Thai government, describing Thai government and administration, history, culture, education, transportation, science, medicine, etc. A useful, if by nature uncritical, bench mark sketch of conditions in Thailand shortly before the end of the era of the absolute monarchy.

Siam: Nature and Industry. Bangkok: Ministry of Commerce and Communications, 1930. 315 pages.

This collection of twenty-two chapters on geography, geology, transportation and communications, the economy, etc., supplements the above-cited *Siam: General and Medical Features*. A useful source of data on various aspects of pre-revolutionary Thailand.

Sirisumpundh, Kasem. "Emergence of the Modern National State in Burma and Thailand." Unpublished Ph.D. dissertation, University of Wisconsin, 1962. 407 pages.

An historical survey and analysis of the development of the contemporary Thai nation-state. Some broad consideration of military and religious influences; a realistic assessment of the basic character of the Thai political system; and some suggestive distinctions between the Thai and Burmese cases.

Srivisarn Vacha, Phya. "Kingship in Siam." *Journal of the Siam Society*, July, 1954, pp. 1-10.

A brief sketch, interesting partly because in the latter 1960's the author served as an assistant to the Prime Minister and as rector of the University of Chiengmai.

Thompson, Virginia. *Thailand, the New Siam*. New York: Macmillan, 1941. 865 pages.

Dated, but remains a source of general information about pre-war diplomacy, modernization, education, government, and politics. Includes a variety of impressionistic interpretations.

Vella, Walter F. *Siam Under Rama III, 1824-1851*. New York: J. J. Augustin, for the Association for Asian Studies, 1957. 180 pages.

A valuable study by a specialist in Thai history. Drawn largely from Thai sources, this work documents the kingship as it was exercised by Rama III. It also provides a discerning portrait of Thailand's encounter with the West in the second quarter of the nineteenth century.

Wales, H. G. Quaritch. *Ancient Siamese Government and Administration*. London: Bernard Quaritch, 1934. Reissued, New York: Paragon Book Reprint, 1956. 206 pages.

The best available English-language source on government in traditional Thailand. Some of Wales' interpretations are open to challenge; for example, his ascribing virtually unlimited power to the king.

Wales, H. G. Quaritch. *Siamese State Ceremonies: Their History and Function*. London: Bernard Quaritch, 1931. 326 pages.

Describes a variety of ceremonies connected with the traditional kingship, related to agriculture, aimed at propitiation of spirits, etc. Also includes much information on the organization and functions of Thai monarchical government.

Wood, W. A. R. *A History of Siam, From the Earliest Times to the Year A.D. 1781, With a Supplement Dealing with More*

Recent Events. London: Unwin, 1926. 294 pages. Revised edition, Bangkok: Siam Barnakich Press, 1933. 300 pages.

A useful and substantial outline of Thai history drawn from ancient chronicles.

Wright, Arnold (ed.). *Twentieth Century Impressions of Siam.* London: Lloyds Great Britain Publishing Company, 1908. 302 pages.

This official volume contains a valuable collection of statements on various aspects of Thai government written by the officials in charge and by foreign advisors. Many of the articles are first-rate descriptions of achievements during the reign of King Chulalongkorn.

Wyatt, David K. *The Politics of Reform in Thailand: Education in the Reign of King Chulalongkorn.* New Haven and London: Yale University Press, 1969.

This study of educational reform in the Fifth Reign of the Bangkok Period (1868-1910) focuses on one aspect of modernization. Examines the roles of the King, his advisors, and professional educators in formulating and directing a program of ambitious educational reform, especially in the period 1898-1910. The project involved both the problem of priorities in a situation of restricted economic and human resources, and the problem of generational and tactical conflict within a rapidly changing elite.

Wyatt, David K., and Constance M. Wilson. "Thai Historical Materials in Bangkok." *Journal of Asian Studies,* November, 1965, pp. 105-118.

A very useful survey of Thai historical materials located in Bangkok, with specific information concerning the nature, origin, extent, location, and accessibility of materials.

2. Thailand and the West

Burney, H. (Envoy to the Court of Siam). *The Burney Papers.* 5 vols. Bangkok: Vajiranana National Library, 1910-1914.

An extensive compilation of official documents and letters between Great Britain and Siam from 1825-1850, one of the decisive periods in Thailand's diplomatic history. Contains documents concerning straits settlements, factory records, and the secret Bengal political consultations. Volume V deals with British policy from the establishment of Penang to 1842; written by Burney and Major James Low, it provides an interesting account of the 1838 Siamese-Malay War and the events surrounding the Malacca Straits settlement.

Collis, Maurice. *Siamese White*. London: Faber and Faber, 1936. 230 pages.

A lively and readable account of the Siamese adventures of Samuel White, a one-time member of the British East India Company establishment who turned adventurer and became involved with Constance Phaulkon, the Greek "prime minister" of Thailand until 1688. A personalized historical account drawn from official sources.

Damrong Rajanubhab, Prince. "The Introduction of Western Culture in Siam." *Journal of the Siam Society*, vol. 20. no. 2, 1926, p. 89 ff.

A brief account of some episodes in Thai-Western relations, by a distinguished Thai statesman and scholar. Reprinted in *Relationship with Portugal, Holland, and the Vatican: Selected Articles from the Journal of the Siam Society, Volume VII*, pp. 1-12.

Drans, Jean, and Henri Bernard, S. J. *Memoire du Père de Beze sur la vie de Constance Phaulkon, Premier Ministre du roi de Siam, Phra Narai et sa triste fin*. Tokyo: Presses Salesiennes, 1947. 282 pages.

Father de Beze's memoir was written about 1689, the year after Phaulkon's violent death. It is published here with a number of pieces of correspondence by, to, or concerning Phaulkon, with a brief introductory essay, a table of corrections of the de Beze mss., and an index.

Kaochareon, Rapee. "The Use of Foreign Advisors and Officials in the Thai Civil Service During Rama V's Through VIII's Reigns." Unpublished Master's thesis, University of New Hampshire, 1963. 313 pages.

Foreign officials and advisors were vital contributors to Thai survival, beginning with the last half of the nineteenth century. This is a detailed survey of their numbers and services, indicating that during the transitional era of administrative reform they literally managed and operated many parts of the emerging bureaucracy.

McFarland, Bertha Blount. *McFarland of Siam.* New York: Vantage Press, 1958. 313 pages.

　　The biography of a man belonging to a missionary family who made significant contributions to medicine, education, and Western technology. Captures the flavor and spirit of the missionary impact during the latter nineteenth and the early twentieth centuries.

Martin, James V., Jr. "A History of the Diplomatic Relations Between Siam and the United States of America, 1933-1939, 1939-1948." See Section C-6.

Modelski, George (ed.). *SEATO: Six Studies.* See Section C-4.

Records of the Relations Between Siam and Foreign Countries in the 17th Century (copied from papers preserved at the India Office). 5 vols. Bangkok: Vajiranana National Library, 1915-1921.

　　A useful official source concerning seventeenth-century diplomacy.

Relationship with Portugal, Holland and the Vatican: Selected Articles from the Journal of the Siam Society, Volume VII. Bangkok: The Siam Society, 1959. 276 pages.

　　A number of articles dealing with sixteenth and seventeenth century Western relations with Thailand, in one of a series of reprint volumes brought out by the Siam Society beginning in 1954.

Relationship with France, England, and Denmark: Selected Articles from the Journal of the Siam Society, Volume VIII. Bangkok: The Siam Society, 1959. 288 pages.

　　A compilation of ten articles by l'Abbé de Choisy, W. E. Hutchinson, Erik Seidenfaden, D. G. E. Hall, and others, concerning Siam's seventeenth and nineteenth-century military and diplomatic relations with France, Denmark, and England. Includes W. E. Hutchinson's "The Four French State Manuscripts Relating to Embassies Between France and Siam in the 17th Century," and Seidenfaden's "Early Trade Relations Between Denmark and Siam."

Sayre, Francis Bowes. "The Passing of Extraterritoriality in Siam." *American Journal of International Law,* January, 1928, pp. 70-88.

　　Sketches the extraterritoriality provisions of Thai-Western treaties from the mid-nineteenth century, and describes the diplomatic action which led to the elimination of extraterritoriality provisions by the 1920's. The author, serving as advisor to the Thai Minister of Foreign Affairs, was a participant in the latter treaty negotiations.

Siam: Treaties with Foreign Powers, 1920-1927. Bangkok: Royal Siamese Government, 1928. 280 pages.

Edited by Phya Kalyan Maitri (Francis Bowes Sayre), this is a collection, in English, of the important treaties that redefined Thai-Western relations, abrogating all former treaties, eliminating extraterritoriality, and re-establishing Thailand's fiscal autonomy. The treaties were signed with Belgium, Denmark, France, Germany, Great Britain, Italy, Japan, Netherlands, Norway, Portugal, Spain, Sweden, and the United States.

Tarling, Nicholas. "Siam and Sir James Brooke." *Journal of the Siam Society,* November, 1960, pp. 43-72.

An interesting account of an early nineteenth-century episode. Discusses the Thai strategy of offering economic concessions during the period preceding the Bowring Treaty of 1854.

Vella, Walter F. *The Impact of the West on Government in Thailand.* Berkeley and Los Angeles: University of California Press, 1955. 410 pages.

Examines the changes in Thai government in the past century in terms of the adaptation of Western ideas, techniques, and institutions. The author systematically traces the political impact of the West, but concludes that "the mass of the Thai population has been little affected by Western ideas on government...."

Vella, Walter F. *Siam Under Rama III, 1824-1851.* See Section B-1.

Young, Kenneth T. "The Special Role of American Advisers in Thailand, 1902-1949." See Section C-6.

C.
CONTEMPORARY POLITICS

The historical past is linked intimately with the present in Thailand. Today's bureaucracy, for example, is an outgrowth of the great reformation of King Chulalongkorn and the events that followed it. The items in this section, however, focus upon the contemporary era, which has so far been the subject of relatively few systematic and system-wide political studies.

This section is divided into six parts: (1) political leaders and the political system; (2) interests and associations; (3) law, justice, and the courts; (4) the military, national security, and communism; (5) subnational government — an awkward term, but one more appropriate than "local government" for Thailand; and (6) contemporary diplomacy and international relations. Relevant material will also be found in other sections, particularly among the histories cited in Section A, as well as in the social structure and social change literature cited in Section G-4.

The standard general study of contemporary Thai politics is David Wilson's *Politics in Thailand*, published in 1962. A growing number of studies of a more specialized nature, however, have appeared in recent years. The study by Fred Riggs, *Thailand: The Modernization of a Bureaucratic Polity*, is perhaps the best example of this type. Riggs describes and analyzes the changing structure of Thai politics and the central place of what he calls the "bureaucratic polity" in the political system.

Studies about interest groups and the Thai legal system remain comparatively rare. This paucity, in Western-language studies at least, marks an area of opportunity — and need — for future research. The Thai political system differs considerably from systems characterized by the existence and ordered operation of political interest groups. It also manifests the working of forms of authority not consistent with overt, systematic interest mobilization. The Chinese are, in a sense, a significant "interest," and among the Chinese exist a number of associations which function somewhat as interest groups. Yet political interest groups in the Western sense are not vital elements in Thai politics.

The literature on military affairs, national security, and communism is of varying quality — indeed, much of it is relatively poor. At one extreme is the recent rash of studies which purport to compare present national security conditions in Thailand with those of Vietnam some years ago. Few, if any, of these studies are convincingly comparative. The subsection treating this literature also contains several examples of the research output of the American military (or its contractors) in Thailand, which tends to be encyclopedic rather than analytical. The studies that attempt to gauge the role of the military in the political life of Thailand, while necessarily somewhat speculative (military expenditures and military manpower data are not public information in Thailand), are nonetheless interesting. The book by Morris Janowitz, *The Military in the Political Development of New Nations* is a general study of the role of the military as a modernizing force in the poor countries; David Wilson's article in the book edited by John J. Johnson considers the place of the military in Thai politics. Communism in Thailand is usually treated as one subpart of communism in Asia, often on the dubious assumption that Asian communism is a unified thing, or as a phenomenon of the Northeast or Southern provinces. Very little in the way of "hard" information is available to support these assumptions.

The literature on subnational government covers a broad spectrum, from surveys of provincial government to village studies. The latter is impressive literature, reflecting the modern social scientists' concern for precision and analytical rigor, which are easier to attain at the village level, and the recognition by both social scientists and funding agencies that the rural areas are critical elements in national development. The study of a Thai-Lao village in northeastern Thailand by Charles Keyes is a fine example of this "new" literature. (See also Section G-1 for items on rural and village life and affairs.) While there is no really good study of metropolitan Bangkok, Thailand's only metropolis, T. G. McGee's *The Southeast Asian City* is a useful study of the principal cities of Southeast Asia — Bangkok, of course, being one.

The literature on contemporary diplomacy and international relations suffers from an almost total reliance on secondary sources. Practically all of it is written from the perspective of the Western observer concerned primarily with the place of Thailand in the struggle for power in Asia.

1. Political Leaders and the Political System

Ayal, Eliezer B. "Public Policies in Thailand Under the Constitutional Regime: A Case Study of an Underdeveloped Country." Unpublished Ph.D. dissertation, Cornell University, 1961. 350 pages.

An analysis of economic policy and policy-making in Thailand from 1932-1957, providing information on economic history and economic aspects of Thai politics during that period.

Coast, John. *Some Aspects of Siamese Politics.* New York: Institute of Pacific Relations, 1953. 58 pages.

A readable, journalistic account of political developments in Thailand from 1932 to 1952, with a first-hand account of some of former Premier Pibul's bizarre attempts to promote Westernization and nationalism.

Coughlin, Richard J. *Double Identity: The Chinese in Modern Thailand.* See Section G-4.

Darling, Frank C. "Marshal Sarit and Absolutist Rule in Thailand." *Pacific Affairs,* December, 1960, pp. 347-360.

This article is interesting in that it views the rule of former Prime Minister Sarit as a reversion to the pre-1932 style of government.

Darling, Frank C. "Modern Politics in Thailand." *The Review of Politics,* April, 1962, pp. 163-182.

An examination of Thailand's recent political past, along with an assessment based upon certain highly subjective assumptions: that at the end of World War II there may have been an alternative to the re-establishment of political control based upon military power; and that Thailand should be moving in the direction of a constitutional democratic state; but that this potential trend may be thwarted by the persistence of military leadership.

Evers, Hans-Dieter, and T. H. Silcock. "Elites and Selection," in T. H. Silcock (ed.), *Thailand: Social and Economic Studies in Development.* Canberra: Australian National University Press, 1967, pp. 84-104.

A good description and analysis of the selection, composition, and development of military, bureaucratic, Chinese, and other Thai elite groups. Analyzes inter-elite group relationships and the possible effects of these relationships upon economic development in Thailand. A selective review of the literature (Embree, Hanks, Mosel, Kaufman, Skinner, Textor, Sharp, and others) on the Thai social system.

Hanks, Lucien M. "American Aid Is Damaging Thai Society." See Section G-1.

Hindley, Donald. "Thailand: The Politics of Passivity." *Pacific Affairs*, Fall, 1968, pp. 355-371.

An interesting and informative essay which attempts to account for political passivity of Thai non-elite groups: peasantry, bureaucracy, and the commercial middle class (see Evers, cited above). Two kinds of explanations are offered. The first examines the extent to which Thailand has experienced conditions that have impelled significant groups in other countries into active opposition to an entrenched and resistant regime. The second identifies those characteristics of the Thai world view which discourage political action.

Huff, Lee. "The Thai Movile Development Unit Program," in Peter Kunstradter (ed.), *Southeast Asian Tribes, Minorities, and Nations*. Princeton: Princeton University Press, 1967, pp. 425-486.

A detailed evaluation of the Mobile Development Units program. The MDU program is one of a number of rural-oriented programs (Community Development, Mobile Information teams, Accelerated Rural Development, and the Developing Democracy Program) designed to improve relations between the central government and Thai peasants by upgrading rural conditions of life.

Keyes, Charles F. *Local Leadership in Rural Thailand*. Los Angeles: Academic Advisory Council for Thailand, University of California at Los Angeles, 1969. 50 pages.

This paper, presented at a Conference on Local Authority in Thailand, systematically distinguishes different types of local leaders, and contains a perceptive analysis of variations in the articulation of official government and peasant communities. Analyzes the impact of inadequate integration of peasant and administrative systems in typical Central Thai villages. A seminal statement.

MacDonald, Alexander. *Bangkok Editor*. See Section A.

Mokarapong, Thawatt. "The June Revolution of 1932 in Thailand:

A Study in Political Behavior." Unpublished Ph.D. dissertation, Indiana University, 1962. 308 pages.

A detailed description of the revolution, the revolutionary leaders, their aims, and the outcome of the overthrow of the monarchy. An authoritative source of information on the *coup* and the members of the revolutionary factions.

Mosel, James N. "Thai Administrative Behavior." See Section D-1.

Nairn, Ronald C. *International Aid to Thailand: The New Colonialism.* See Section F-2.

Neuchterlein, Donald E. "Thailand after Sarit." *Asian Survey,* May, 1964, pp. 842-850.

An interim analysis of the shifting power configuration at the top of the Thai system. Asserts that the king serves as more than a national symbol — i.e., that he also plays a critical part in legitimizing any group which would command the government. Discusses the rumored role of the king in the transfer of power to Prime Minister Sarit and in the stabilization of the position of Sarit's successor, Field Marshal Thanom.

Phillips, Herbert P. "The Election Ritual in a Thai Village." *Journal of Social Issues,* December, 1958, pp. 36-50.

A discerning examination of the forces which produced voting behavior in a Thai village. The widespread turnout in the village was found to be a response to traditional social force and bureaucratic authority, rather than an expression of political interest.

Pickerell, Albert, and Daniel E. Moore. "Elections in Thailand." *Far Eastern Survey,* June and July, 1957, pp. 92-97, 103-111.

A journalistic account of events during the national elections of February, 1957.

Pye, Lucien W. *Southeast Asian Political Systems.* Englewood Cliffs: Prentice-Hall, 1967. 98 pages.

An attempt to analyze Southeast Asian political systems in terms of political foundations, political dynamics, and the formal decision-making organs of government on the input side, and short and long-run governmental efficiency and performance on the output side. The Thai data are neither as current nor as accurate as they might be; the Thai analysis is perhaps the least satisfactory.

Riggs, Fred W. *Thailand: The Modernization of a Bureaucratic Polity.* Honolulu: East-West Center Press, 1966. 470 pages.

Systematically examines contemporary Thai government as a "bureaucratic polity." Using the governmental promotion of rice production and control over various apsects of rice marketing as a focus, Riggs traces changing patterns of government and government-social systems relations. A detailed description and analysis of the Thai political decisional structure as of the late 1950's.

Rozental, Alek A. "Branch Banking in Thailand." See Section E-1.

Sharp, Lauriston. "Peasants and Politics in Thailand." *Far Eastern Survey,* September, 1950, pp. 157-161.

An examination of the political attitudes of some Thai peasants toward the Bangkok government. Although now out-of-date, it remains important because it contains many of the ideas about peasant relationships with the Thai government that have since become unquestioned stereotypes.

Silcock, T. H. "Money and Banking." See Section E-1.

Simmonds, Stuart. "Thailand — A Conservative State," in Saul Rose (ed.), *Politics in Southern Asia.* New York: St. Martin's Press, 1963, pp. 119-142.

A resume of recent Thai domestic and diplomatic history and an impressionistic assessment of the authoritarian basis of Thai politics. Simmonds opines that the political characteristics of contemporary Thailand are acceptable to most Thais and consistent with continuing economic development, but suggests that the future may bring demands for broader political participation.

Singh, L. P. *The Politics of Economic Cooperation in Asia. A Study of Asian International Organizations.* Columbia: University of Missouri Press, 1966. 271 pages.

The obstacles to economic development in Asia, the author contends, are psychological, economic, and political — most of all, political. This is largely a study of organizations: ECAFE, Colombo Plan, SEATO, the Association of Southeast Asia (ASA), and the Asian Productivity Organization.

Sivaram, M. *The New Siam in the Making.* Bangkok: Stationers Printing Press, 1936. 158 pages.

A subjective examination of the efforts to erect a stable political structure in the politically fluid years following the 1932 revolution.

Sutton, Joseph L. "Political and Administrative Leadership," in Joseph L. Sutton (ed.), *Problems of Politics and Administration in Thailand*. Bloomington: Institute of Training for Public Service, Indiana University, 1962, pp. 1-22.

 A brief subjective essay about the influence of Buddhism and the tradition of the absolutist state on Thai political and administrative leadership.

Thomas, M. Ladd. *Socio-Economic Approach to Political Integration of the Thai-Islam: An Appraisal*. DeKalb: Center for Southeast Asian Studies, Northern Illinois University, 1969. 27 pages.

 Based upon field work during 1966-1968, the study assesses Thai government efforts to promote political integration, identifies basic limitations to achieve such goals, offers recommendations, and concludes that by adroit and patient efforts the Thai government might, over two or three decades, achieve a substantial practical identification of Thai-Islam individuals and communities with the Thai government.

Tulyathorn, Prasit. "The First Decade of Constitutional Government in Thailand." Unpublished Master's thesis, University of Hawaii, 1964. 87 pages.

 Political history (1932-1942), containing policy changes of successive cabinets and some translated government statements.

Tunsiri, Vichai. "The Social Background and the Legislative Recruitment of the Thai Members of Parliament and Their Political Consequences." Unpublished Ph.D. dissertation, Indiana University, 1971. 300 pages.

 Analyzes relation of legislators' behavior to their socio-economic backgrounds, 1933-1970. Presents observed patterns and an empirically-grounded model of Thai legislative behavior.

Wilson, David A. *Politics in Thailand*. Ithaca: Cornell University Press, 1962. 307 pages.

 Authoritative study of modern Thai government and politics. Wilson's views of the Thai political leadership coincide with those of Riggs and Mosel, but his study covers more, and amounts to a survey of the contemporary political system.

Wilson, David A. "Thailand," in George McT. Kahin (ed.), *Governments and Politics of Southeast Asia*. Revised edition. Ithaca: Cornell University Press, 1964, pp. 3-72.

 An updated version of Wilson's lengthier work, cited above.

Wilson, David A. "Thailand: A New Leader." *Asian Survey*, February, 1964, pp. 171-175.
  A brief survey of political conditions at the end of the Sarit regime and the beginning of the premiership of Marshal Thanom.

Wilson, David A., and Herbert P. Phillips. "Elections and Parties in Thailand." *Far Eastern Survey*, August, 1958, pp. 113-119.
  Places the election process in its larger political and social context. (See also Phillips, cited above.)

Yang, Shu-Chin. *A Multiple Exchange Rate System: An Appraisal of Thailand's Experience, 1946-1955*. See Section E-1.

Young, Stephen B. "The Northeastern Thai Village: A Non-Participatory Democracy." *Asian Survey*, November, 1968, pp. 873-886.
  Examines political behavior in four northeastern villages — a large and prosperous village in Udorn province and three small, isolated, poor villages in Mahasarakham province — and concludes that villagers in all four conceive the legitimate role of government to be very limited.

2. Interests and Associations

Atibaed, Sanee. "Occupational Restriction Affecting Aliens in Thailand Since World War I." Unpublished Master's thesis, 1960. Bangkok: Institute of Public Administration, Thammasat University. 87 pages.
  A summarization of official police and legislative measures aimed at restricting the access of aliens to certain occupations. As the measures have been largely directed against the Chinese, this formal study is relevant to an examination of relationships between Chinese and the Thai government.

Dulayachinda, Medhi. "The Development of Labor Legislation in Thailand." *International Labor Review*, vol. 60, 1949, pp. 467-486.
  A sketch of Thailand's labor laws. Discusses governmental efforts to use law as an instrument for promoting labor welfare without creating a politically effective labor group.

Riggs, Fred W. *Census and Notes on Clientele Groups in Thai Politics and Administration.* Bloomington: Institute of Training for Public Service, Indiana University, 1963. 42 pages.

> A summary of voluntary associations found in Thailand in 1958, with detailed notes, based upon interviews, on some of these associations. In addition, there is a summary description of mass media in Thailand as of 1957.

Riggs, Fred W. "Interest and Clientele Groups," in Joseph L. Sutton (ed.), *Problems of Politics and Administration in Thailand.* Bloomington: Institute of Training for Public Service, Indiana University, 1962, pp. 152-192.

> A brief description and analysis of the character and functions of interest groups in the Thai political system.

Riggs, Fred W. "A Model for the Study of Thai Society." *Thai Journal of Public Administration,* April, 1961, pp. 83-120.

> Although this is essentially a conceptual scheme, it takes into account the nature and functioning of interests and interest groups in the Thai political sphere.

3. Law, Justice, and the Courts

Darling, Frank C. "Aspects of Thai Law." (Paper delivered at the Midwest Conference on Asian Affairs, University of Kansas, Lawrence, Kansas, November 10-11, 1967.) 26 pages.

> Sketches the development of Thai law. Notes that despite radical changes which have taken place in the Thai legal system, it remains a mixture of the traditional and the modern.

Dulayachinda, Medhi. "The Development of Labor Legislation in Thailand." See Section C-2.

Lingat, Robert. "Evolution of the Conception of Law in Burma and Siam." *Journal of the Siam Society,* January, 1950, pp. 9-31.

> Describes the Burmese and Siamese view of law as synonymous with a notion of a universal moral order, and asserts that this view imposes and reflects limitations upon rulers, in the form of their own conception of their obligations and in the form of general expectations within the society.

Lyman, Albert. "The Judicial System in Thailand." *Journal of the Bar Association of the District of Columbia,* February, 1955, pp. 85-92.

A brief sketch of the Thai judicial system by an American lawyer practicing in Bangkok, with emphasis on jurisdiction. Essentially concerned with formal characteristics of the judicial system.

Revenue Laws and Their Administration. Bangkok: Ministry of Finance, 1955. 250 pages.

A consultant's report prepared by Howell & Company. Essentially a study of revenue administration, but also an interesting and revealing description of the Thai tax structure and revenue law administration as of the early 1950's.

Sayre, Francis Bowes. "The Passing of Extraterritoriality in Siam." See Section B-2.

Van Roy, Edward. "Economic Dualism and Economic Change Among the Hill Tribes of Thailand." See Section G-4.

Wit, Daniel. Labor Law and Practice in Thailand. U.S. Bureau of Labor Statistics. Washington, D.C.: Government Printing Office, 1964. 53 pages.

A descriptive background report on labor and labor law.

Wood, W. A. R. *Notes on the Jurisdiction of Consular and International Courts in Siam.* Bloomington: Department of Political Science, Indiana University, October, 1964. 19 pages.

Personal account of the development of consular and international courts in Thailand, from the first British consular court in 1865 to the end of extraterritoriality in 1925. The author was for many years involved in the administration of the British courts in Thailand.

4. The Military, National Security, and Communism

Blakeslee, D. J., L. W. Huff, and R. W. Kickert. *Village Security Pilot Study.* Bangkok: Joint Thai-U.S. Military Research and Development Center, May, 1965. 387 pages.

An attempt to develop a data base of information relevant to village security in remote areas of Thailand. Forty villages in Northeast Thailand were studied in terms of (a) general and locational data (names of village officials, population, latitude and longitude, police posts, etc.); (b) defense perimeter data (areas and village shapes); (c) physical structural characteristics (local industries, fuel storage, etc.); (d) transportation; and (e) topographic features.

Block, Edward Leigh. "Accelerated Rural Development: A Counter-Insurgency Program in Northeast Thailand." Unpublished Master's thesis, Northern Illinois University, 1968. 105 pages.

A case study of the American-sponsored Accelerated Rural Development (ARD) program for Northeast Thailand, intended to counter insurgency by improving rural living standards. Concludes that while the ARD program may conceivably be effective in the long run, its current security orientation and absence of concern for felt needs in the villages, are not promising signs.

Brimmell, J. H. *Communism in South East Asia, A Political Analysis.* Oxford: Oxford University Press, for the Royal Institute of International Affairs, 1959. 415 pages.

Communism is considered by the author to be by far the most dynamic political influence at work within Southeast Asia, although the movement in Thailand was in 1959 apparently feeble. The pattern of communist organization in Thailand is described.

Buss, Claude A. *The Arc of Crisis.* See Section A.

Changwad Handbook on Changwad Nakhon Phanom. See Section C-5.

Clubb, Oliver E., Jr. *The United States and the Sino-Soviet Bloc in Southeast Asia.* See Section C-6.

Coward, H. Roberts. *Military Technology in Developing Countries.* Cambridge: Center for International Studies, Massachusetts Institute of Technology, 1964. 51 pages + appendices.

A source of data and estimates concerning the Thai military forces, including "most current available data" on the size of the Thai armed forces, comparative estimates and projections of the ratio of Thai forces to the Thai population, and relation of the Thai defense budget to GNP. Also contains manpower and defense budget extrapolation from 1961 through 1975.

Girling, J. C. S. "Northeast Thailand: Tomorrow's Viet Nam?" *Foreign Affairs*, January, 1968, pp. 388-397.

Concludes that while there are historic, economic, and political reasons for insurgency in Northeast Thailand, the situation is not comparable to that of Vietnam.

Janowitz, Morris. *The Military in the Political Development of New Nations: An Essay in Comparative Analysis*. Chicago: University of Chicago Press, 1964. 134 pages.

Sketches a variety of types of civil-military relations in the developing nations and formulates a number of hypotheses about the political capacity of the military to govern and to modernize. Passing description of the Thai military.

Modelski, George (ed.). *SEATO: Six Studies*. Melbourne: Australian National University Press, 1962. 302 pages.

These studies have one common denominator — they all see SEATO as a Western Great Power arrangement. Three describe the place of the small member-states in the alliance; two deal with policies of India and China *vis-à-vis* SEATO; one describes the role of the Great Powers in Asian trade relationships.

Perlo, Victor, and Kumar Goshal. *Bitter End in Southeast Asia*. New York: Marzani and Munsell, 1964. 128 pages.

An attack on American policy in Vietnam and SEATO. SEATO is described as "A Dulles Nightmare."

SEATO Record. See Section I-2.

Stanton, Edwin F. "Communist Pressures in Thailand." *Current History*, February, 1960, pp. 102-109.

A former American ambassador to Thailand sketches the apparent dimensions of communist power and influence within the country as of 1960.

Warner, Denis. "Aggression by Seepage in Northeast Thailand." *Reporter*, October 25, 1962, pp. 33-37.

A journalistic discussion of communist infiltration in rural Northeast Thailand. This and two other complementary articles on Thailand appear in Warner's *Reporting Southeast Asia* (Sydney: Angus and Robertson, 1966).

Wilson, David A. "The Military in Thai Politics," in John J. Johnson (ed.), *The Role of the Military in Underdeveloped Countries*. Princeton: Princeton University Press, 1962, pp. 253-275.

Traces the historical background of the military in Thai politics: the emergence of a modern professional military apparatus; military participation in the 1932 revolution; and the military envelopment of Thai politics in the years which followed. Suggests that the army fills a political vacuum, exercising power rather than authority, and that it works to help preserve the political *status quo*.

Wilson, David A. "Thailand and Marxism," in Frank N. Trager (ed.), *Marxism in Southeast Asia: A Study of Four Countries.* Stanford: Stanford University Press, 1959, pp. 58-101.

Asserts a limited significance for Marxism in Thailand, because political, social, and cultural factors have made the Marxist appeal one of small relevance to Thais.

5. Subnational Government

Amphoe-Tambon Statistical Directory of 14 ARD Changwads. Bangkok: Department of Local Administration, National Statistical Office, U.S. Agency for International Development, March, 1967. 301 pages.

Maps and tabular data on amphoes and tambons in the fourteen provinces earmarked for special assistance by the Agency for International Development-Department of Local Administration ARD (Accelerated Rural Development) program. Data on number of villages, households, schools, teachers, pupils, crop holdings, rice production, land in crops, land under irrigation, rice planted.

Changwad Handbook on Changwad Nakhon Phanom. 6 vols. Bangkok: Joint Thai-U.S. Military Research and Development Center, prepared for the Advanced Research Projects Agency, Office of the Secretary of Defense, Washington, D.C., 1967 and 1968.

A detailed compilation of data on the physical, social, economic and political characteristics of this northeastern province. Volume I: Physical Environment; Volume II: Social Environment; Volume III: Economic Environment; Volume IV: Public Administration Environment; Volume V: Summary and Bibliography; Volume VI: Special Village Maps. Volumes are descriptive and encyclopedic rather than analytic. (In English and Thai.)

de Young, John E. *Village Life in Modern Thailand.* See Section G-1.

Fraser, Thomas M., Jr. *Fishermen of South Thailand: The Malay Villagers.* New York: Holt, Rinehart and Winston, 1966. 110 pages.

A shorter version of the author's *Rusembilan: A Malay Fishing Village in Southern Thailand,* cited below.

Fraser, Thomas M., Jr. *Rusembilan: A Malay Fishing Village in Southern Thailand.* Ithaca: Cornell University Press, 1960. 281 pages.

This is a study of the Malay fishing village of Rusembilan on the Gulf of Thailand in Pattani province — one of the four predominantly Malay provinces in the south of Thailand. The first published account of any Malay community in Thailand, this study of the cultural behavior of a Moslem-Malay peasant group is well done.

Hanna, Willard A. *A Series of Reports on Thailand.* New York: American Universities Field Staff, 1965-1966.

This particular set of AUFS reports consists of twenty-five separate documents, of four to sixteen pages each. Fifteen are entitled "Change in Chiengmai." (They are separately subtitled, and identified as Southeast Asia Series, vol. XIII, nos. 2, 3, 5, 6, 8, 9, 10, 12-19. They were issued from February through May, 1965. Together they provide a perceptive portrait of salient features of this northern area.) Five are titled "Peninsular Thailand." (Also separately subtitled, these reports deal with the southernmost provinces. Southeast Asia Series, vol. XIII, nos. 22-26.) A single report sketches a few aspects of change in "Thailand's Strategic Northeast." (Southeast Asia Series, vol. XIV, no. 1, January, 1966. 18 pages.)

Hoath, James R. *Local Government in Thailand — Development Implications.* Bangkok: U.S. Agency for International Development, 1968. 25 pages.

A general discussion of how development is affecting the system of local administration. Describes the general structure of local government and considers ways in which village structures might be used as the locus of developmental efforts.

Horrigan, Frederick James. "Local Government and Administration in Thailand: A Study of Institutions and Their Cultural Setting." Unpublished Ph.D. dissertation, Indiana University, 1959. 338 pages.

Traces the evolution of provincial government, and discusses the structure and general operating characteristics of Thai provincial and subprovincial government as of the latter 1950's.

Horrigan, Frederick James. "Provincial Government and Administration," in Joseph L. Sutton (ed.), *Problems of Politics and Administration in Thailand*. Bloomington: Institute of Training for Public Service, Indiana University, 1962, pp. 41-72.

A short description of provincial and local government, drawn from Horrigan's doctoral dissertation, cited above.

Impact of USOM Support Programs in Changwad Sakon Nakhon. Bangkok: U.S. Agency for International Development, 1967. 138 pages.

Examines the impact of assistance programs in an ARD province upon the attitudes and behavior of rural people. Includes a project-by-project analysis of success in planning and coordination, security, and the satisfaction of village development needs as compared with two control amphurs in which no AID programs exist.

Janlekha, Kamol Odd. *A Study of the Economy of a Rice-Growing Village in Central Thailand*. See Section E-1.

Judd, Laurence C. "A Study of the Cultural Organization of Tong Taa Village in Thailand." Unpublished Master's thesis, Cornell University, 1954.

A brief, discerning, unpretentious study of Tong Taa village, near Pitsanuloke, by a missionary in the area. Covers geography and history, population, education, socio-economic patterns, health conditions, recreation, religion, leadership, and apparent patterns of change.

Karnjanaprakorn, Choop. *Community Development and Local Government in Thailand*. See Section G-1.

Karnjanaprakorn, Choop. *Municipal Government in Thailand as an Institution and Process of Self-Government*. Bangkok: Institute of Public Administration, Thammasat University, 1962. 253 pages.

A reprint of a doctoral dissertation submitted to Indiana University, 1959. The author participated in drafting the Municipalities Act in 1952 and has had extensive personal experience in local government in Thailand.

Kaufman, Howard K. *Bangkhuad: A Community Study in Thailand*.

New York: J. J. Augustin, for the Association for Asian Studies, 1960. 235 pages.

A perceptive, detailed, and readable anthropological study of a village in the central basin of Thailand. Describes the pattern of daily life, the typical life cycle, the community structure, economy, government, and educational and religious institutions. Informative appendices, including the "Ten Most Common Proverbs Used by the Farmers of Bangkhuad," and a list of thirty common superstitions. See also Section G-1.

Keyes, Charles F. *Isan: Regionalism in Northeastern Thailand.* See Section G-1.

Keyes, Charles F. "Peasant and Nation: Thai-Lao Village in a Thai State." Unpublished Ph.D. dissertation, Cornell University, 1966. 384 pages.

An anthropological case study of the village of Ban Nong, Mahasarakam province, northeastern Thailand, which offers not only systematic information about socio-cultural characteristics of the village, but an extensive orientation of the village within its larger setting — bureaucratic and political, educational, religious, economic, and informational. Perceptive observations include a comprehensive portrait of the structure and process of education in the village and of the impact of school teachers upon the shaping of villagers' views of the larger world.

Keyfitz, Nathan. "Political-Economic Aspects of Urbanization in South and Southeast Asia," in Philip Hauser and Leo Schnore (eds.), *The Study of Urbanization.* New York: Wiley, 1965, pp. 265-309.

Examines the political-economic relationship between urban and rural areas, asserting that "an imbalance in the exchange of goods between city and countryside is made up by the exercise of power on the part of the city, and that the decline in food surplus available in the countryside [due to population growth] attenuates the base which the city had in colonial and precolonial times." A worthy contribution to a valuable book.

Kingshill, Konrad. *Ku Daeng — The Red Tomb. A Village Study in Northern Thailand.* Chiengmai and Bangkok: The Prince Royal's College, 1960. Distributed by The Siam Society, Bangkok. 310 pages.

A socio-anthropological survey based on extended residence in this particular village. Describes the economy, family, educational patterns, government, religion, and other social patterns. Vivid and informative.

Litchfield, Whiting, Boune & Associates. *Greater Bangkok Plan.* Bangkok: Ministry of Interior, 1960. 210 pages.

A report of a two-year study of the problems and prospects of the Greater Bangkok metropolitan area, by a consulting firm. Includes descriptive material on characteristics of the nation's only metropolitan area.

Luykx, Nicolaas G. M. "Some Comparative Aspects of Rural Public Institutions in Thailand, the Philippines, and Viet Nam." Unpublished Ph.D. dissertation, Cornell University, 1962. 905 pages.

Includes a description through case studies of formal and actual patterns of rural local government in parts of Thailand.

McGee, T. G. *The Southeast Asian City: A Social Geography of the Primate Cities of Southeast Asia.* New York: Frederick A. Praeger, 1967. 204 pages.

Focuses on the growth, characteristics, and roles of the great cities of Southeast Asia — Bangkok, Rangoon, Singapore, Siagon-Cholon, Djakarta, and Manila. Points to the fact that the economic, political, and social conditions underlying urban growth in these Southeast Asian cities differ greatly from conditions in Western Europe at the time of the first urban explosion. Tables, maps, and a brief but excellent bibliography of Southeast Asian urbanization.

Madge, Charles. *Survey Before Development in Thai Villages.* New York: United Nations Secretariat (U.N. Series on Community Development), 1957. 90 pages. (Also other versions, including one in Thai.)

This study, prepared by a British sociologist, provides valuable material on the social conditions of several rural villages near Ubol. The major purpose of the study, made under the auspices of TUFEC (Thailand-UNESCO Fundamental Education Center), was to determine a sociocultural "baseline" of Northeastern Thai villages before community development programs were introduced.

Madge, Charles. *Village Communities in Northeast Thailand: Survey of the Thailand-UNESCO Fundamental Education Center (TUFEC).* Bangkok: United Nations Technical Assistance Program, 1955. 99 pages.

Madge's final report to the Thai government on the TUFEC

program at Ubol, Northeast Thailand. Describes the social and economic setting and concludes with proposals for community development in the Northeast.

Maynard, Paul, and Charles Murray (eds.). *Thai Local Administration: A Study of Villager Interaction with Community and Amphoe Administration.* Fort Washington, Pennsylvania: Education and Technical Services Division, Philco-Ford Corporation, 1968. 166 pages + 14 appendices.

Prepared for AID-Thailand, this is a substantial field study undertaken in four villages in the northeastern changwad, Nakhon Phanom. Its major conclusions are that villager attitudes toward government have not been highly influenced by developmental activities, that village self-governing capabilities tend to be underestimated, and that village development is adversely affected by existing relations between changwad and amphoe. The study offers impressive and valuable insights into patterns of political organization and behavior at the village level, and rather vivid portraits of village relationships with official government for the four villages in the two amphoe.

Meksawan, Arsa. *The Role of the Provincial Governor in Thailand.* Bangkok: Institute of Public Administration, Thammasat University, 1962. 370 pages. Reissued, 1966.

A reprint of a doctoral dissertation, submitted to Indiana University, 1961. Describes the evolution of the system of provincial government and examines the role of the governor in contemporary Thailand.

Neher, Clark D. *Development in Rural Thailand.* See Section D-1.

Neher, Clark D. "District Level Politics in Thailand." Unpublished Ph.D. dissertation, University of California at Los Angeles, 1969.

A study of decision-making (primarily in the allocation of resources by district officials) at the district level, focusing on three districts in Chiengmai province.

Neher, Clark D. *Rural Thai Government: The Politics of the Budgetary Process.* DeKalb: Center for Southeast Asian Studies, Northern Illinois University, 1970. 60 pages.

Detailed description of the governmental budgetary process in Chieng Mai Province, including the collection and allocation of the local development tax and the actual roles of commune councils, district officers, and provincial authorities. An informed case study of authority patterns in Thai rural local government drawn from the author's dissertation research.

Nims, Cyrus R. *City Planning in Thailand.* Bangkok: U.S. Agency for International Development, 1963. 61 pages.

The final report of the USOM city planning advisor to the Thai government. Reviews and evaluates Thai successes and failures in the field of city planning.

Noranitipandungkarn, Chakrit. *Elites, Power Structure and Politics in Thai Communities.* Bangkok: Research Center, National Institute of Development Administration, 1970. 199 pages.

An elite-community power study of two small urban places, each about 100 kilometers from Bangkok. Interesting, informative, and containing vivid biographical sketches of elite members, this carefully-crafted study reveals a substantial pluralism and dynamism within and among the elite structures. It gives valuable insights into social, cultural, economic, and political factors and their interplay in two municipalities. After the fashion of our times, the title is misleading; the book is about *two* Thai communities.

Pattiya, Akom. "Local Government in Songkhla." Unpublished Master's thesis. Bangkok: Institute of Public Administration, Thammasat University, 1958. 102 pages.

A case study of the formal government of a provincial Thai city. Brief description of Songkhla's relationship to the central government, and of personnel and fiscal administration within the city government.

Phowaathii, Dharmmakhaam. "An Account of Past Events in the Municipalities of Thailand," in *Some Problems in Public Administration in Developing Countries.* Honolulu: East-West Center Press, 1966, pp. 24-43.

A paper presented at the first assembly of the Municipal League in Thailand, held at Chiengmai in 1960; an interesting anecdotal account of some major episodes in the development of municipalities in Thailand from the 1890's into the present era. Suggests the perspective from which some of the Thais involved in it view municipal government.

Piker, Steven. "Sources of Stability and Instability in Rural Thai Society." See Section G-1.

Poowanatnuruk, Prakarn. "The Development of City Zoning in

the Bangkok Metropolitan Area." Unpublished Master's thesis. Bangkok: Institute of Public Administration, Thammasat University, 1960. 133 pages.

A case description, showing the interaction of the Thai government and a city planning consulting firm in evolving an improved land-use plan for the metropolitan area in the late 1950's. An appendix includes translations of the proceedings of a series of conferences on planning and zoning held in the Ministry of Interior.

Ryan, John William. "Municipal Government and Administration," in Joseph L. Sutton (ed.), *Problems of Politics and Administration in Thailand*. Bloomington: Institute of Training for Public Service, Indiana University, 1962, pp. 73-121.

A short study of the development of Thai municipal government, based upon the author's unpublished Ph.D. dissertation on Bangkok government (Indiana University, 1959). Emphasizes the inconsistency between the ideal of local urban self-government and the Thai tradition of national dominance and control.

Sharp, Lauriston, *et al. Siamese Rice Village: A Preliminary Study of Bang Chan, 1948-1949*. See Section G-1.

Silabhundhu, Charoensook. "Study of National Control of Sukhaphiban Finance." Unpublished Master's thesis. Bangkok: Institute of Public Administration, Thammasat University, 1960. 149 pages.

A detailed description of the patterns of financial administration and control of minor urban governmental units sometimes described as "sanitary districts." Some discussion of problems of revenue administration, as well as of actual practice in financial administration.

Sommers, William A. *Report on Amphoe Administration*. Bangkok: U.S. Agency for International Development, 1966. 73 pages.

Includes a description of district administrative organization and administrative problems, and an evaluation of administrative characteristics of the central government mechanism for directing and controlling district administration.

Sommers, William A. *Statistics on Municipal Revenues in Thailand, 1963 to 1966*. Bangkok: U.S. Agency for International Development, October, 1967. n.p., 9 tables.

Statistics on revenues for 120 municipalities, plus population data, ranking of municipalities according to per capita revenue, and a list of sources of municipal revenue.

Sommers, William A. *A Summary of the Budget Process for the Changwad Local Government.* See Section D-3.

Starbird, Ann, et al. *Annotated Bibliography of Northeast Thailand.* See Section H.

"Symposium on Northeast Thailand." See Section G-4.

Vilaichitt, Snit. *Kamnan and Puyaiban: Their Origin, History and Importance to Village Development in Thailand.* See Section D-1.

Wijeyewardene, G. "Some Aspects of Rural Life in Thailand." See Section G-1.

Yatsushiro, Toshio (ed.). *Studies of Northeast Villages in Thailand.* Bangkok: U.S. Agency for International Development, September, 1968. Unpaged.

A two-volume collection of field reports prepared by, or under the direction of, Dr. Yatsushiro when he served on the US-AID mission research staff. Volume I, subtitled "Village Summaries," contains his twenty-five page summary report on attitudes toward security and perceptions of security conditions in seventeen villages in Sakon Nakorn and Mahasarakham provinces, as of 1966 and 1967, plus a summary report on each village by a Thai field investigator. Volume II, "Village Meetings," contains twenty-one transcriptions of conversations with groups of village leaders, a transcription of an interview with a surrendered communist terrorist, an account of a village "brain-washing" episode, background data on six surrendered communist terrorists, and a summary report on village attitudes in Northeast Thailand. Together the volumes present more than eight hundred pages of valuable source material, some in analytic reports and some in field notes. In 1970 Dr. Yatsushiro had completed a yet unpublished monograph, "Northeast Thailand: Its Land, People, and Culture," based partly on these village studies.

Yatsushiro, Toshio. *Village Organization and Leadership in Northeast Thailand.* Bangkok: Department of Community Development, Ministry of Interior, and U.S. Agency for International Development, 1966. 152 pages.

Reports findings of an attitudinal survey of 524 household heads in five villages in the Renu area of Northeast Thailand.

The survey covered village problems and needs, attitudes toward the central government and Western and communist nations, and patterns of village leadership.

6. Contemporary Diplomacy and International Relations

Clubb, Oliver E., Jr. *The United States and the Sino-Soviet Bloc in Southeast Asia.* Washington: The Brookings Institute, 1962. 173 pages.

A survey of Southeast Asian involvement in the confrontation between communist and noncommunist forces. Some discussion of communist pressures in Thailand, but the major value of this work lies in its treatment of the context of Thai diplomacy and Thai foreign relations.

Crosby, Sir Josiah. *Siam: The Crossroads.* See Section B-1.

Crozier, Brian. *Southeast Asia in Turmoil.* See Section A.

Darling, Frank C. *Thailand and the United States.* Washington: Public Affairs Press, 1965. 243 pages.

Detailed information about Thai politics and Thai-U.S. relations in the post-World War II period. Also numerous personal opinions and prescriptions of the author, some of which are quite debatable.

Darling, Frank C. *Thailand: New Challenge and the Struggle for a Political and Economic "Take-Off."* New York: American-Asian Education Exchange, March 1969. 49 pages.

Examines external (China and North Vietnam) and internal (geographic sectionalism and ethnic diversity) threats to Thailand, and Thai efforts to counter these perceived dangers. Argues for a continuation of the current American policy of "containment and construction" in Thailand.

Economic and Technical Cooperation Agreements, 1950-1961. Bangkok: National Economic Development Board, 1961. 169 pages.

A bilingual (Thai-English) record of the formal agreements

providing for economic and technical cooperation between Thailand and other nations, including the United States.

Elsbree, Willard H. *Japan's Role in Southeast Asian Nationalist Movements, 1940 to 1945.* Cambridge: Harvard University Press, 1953. 182 pages.
Relevant to the study of Japanese impact upon Thailand's colonial neighbors at the time of World War II.

Fifield, Russell H. *The Diplomacy of Southeast Asia, 1945-1948.* New York: Harper & Row, 1958. 584 pages.
An excellent guide to the political framework of the region and its literature from 1945-1948. Chapter 7, "Kingdom of Thailand," is a substantial account of Thai foreign relations and foreign policy during that period.

Foreign Affairs Bulletin. See Section I-5.

Fourth Annual Compendium of Assistance to Thailand. Bangkok: Development Assistance Committee, 1966. 97 pages.
A tabular compilation of basic data on foreign aid activities in Thailand, exclusive of military assistance. Sums projects by category: agriculture, education, health and sanitation, industry and technology, and public administration and related. Includes financial data, numbers of experts, students and trainees involved, and in some cases notes on possible future action.

Gordon, Bernard K. *The Dimensions of Conflict in Southeast Asia.* Englewood Cliffs: Prentice-Hall, 1966. 201 pages.
Describes several of the attempts at cooperation among the states of the region. One chapter is devoted to ASA (the Association of Southeast Asia), involving Thailand, Malaysia, and the Philippines. Also describes various intra-regional conflicts: the Philippines' claim to Sabah, the Indonesian-Malaysian confrontation, Cambodia's problems with its neighbors.

Gordon, Bernard K. *Toward Disengagement in Asia: A Strategy for American Foreign Policy.* See Section A.

Halpern, A. M. (ed.). *Policies Toward China: Views from Six Countries.* New York: McGraw-Hill, 1965. 528 pages + appendices.
A valuable and careful inquiry into the foreign policy of a number of nations toward the same set of issues — those posed

by post-war, mainland China. Thirteen substantive chapters deal with individual countries, Thailand included; three focus on clusters of countries.

Inoki, Masamichi. "Japan and the National and Social Revolutions in Southeast Asia: A Policy Proposal." *Japan's Future in Southeast Asia*, Symposium Series II, The Center for Southeast Asian Studies, Kyoto University, July, 1966, pp. 167-174.

Concludes that American policy in Southeast Asia "has not been successful," except with countries, such as Thailand, that have allied themselves with the West.

Landon, Kenneth Perry. "Siam." See Section B-1.

Lomax, Louis E. *Thailand: The War That Is, the War That Will Be.* New York: Random House, 1967. 175 pages.

Argues that the American military assistance program to Thailand is similar to the earlier one in Vietnam and thus the results are likely to be much the same. Superficial and unconvincing.

McLane, Charles B. *Soviet Strategies in Southeast Asia: An Exploration of Eastern Policy under Lenin and Stalin.* Princeton: Princeton University Press, 1966. 563 pages.

Relatively little in this book deals directly with Thailand, though much of it may have implications for Thailand.

Martin, James V., Jr. "A History of the Diplomatic Relations Between Siam and the United States of America, 1933-1939, 1939-1948." 2 vols. Unpublished Ph.D. dissertation, Fletcher School of Law and Diplomacy, 1948.

Detailed and thorough description of Thai-U.S. diplomatic relations during the period indicated.

Martin, James V., Jr. "Thai-American Relations in World War II." *Journal of Asian Studies*, August, 1963, pp. 467-541.

A brief but authoritative account drawn from the above-cited work by Martin.

Modelski, George (ed.). SEATO: Six Studies. See Section C-4.

Montgomery, John D. *The Politics of Foreign Aid: American Experiences in Southeast Asia.* New York: Frederick A. Praeger, 1962. 336 pages.

An analysis of foreign aid as an instrument of foreign policy, with reference to American experience in Burma, Taiwan, Thailand, and Vietnam. Less attention to Thailand than to Taiwan and Vietnam.

Mozingo, David. "Containment in Asia Reconsidered." *World Politics*, April, 1967, pp. 361-377.

Of interest here for its argument that China is willing to live at peace with any Southeast Asian state that does not associate itself closely with the United States. Contends that China's vilification of the Thai government began after the United States was permitted to use Thai territory for American military purposes. (For a contrary view see Gordon's *Toward Disengagement in Asia* in Section A.)

Neuchterlein, Donald E. *Thailand and the Struggle for Southeast Asia*. Ithaca: Cornell University Press, 1965. 279 pages.

A thoughtful, subjective examination of Thailand's foreign relations during and after World War II. Considers Thailand's involvement in SEATO, the Thai posture toward Laos, and Thai-U.S. relations.

Peterson, Alex. "Britain and Siam: The Last Phase." *Pacific Affairs*, December, 1946, pp. 364-372.

An account of negotiations between Britain and Thailand following the Second World War.

Sayre, Francis Bowes. "The Passing of Extraterritoriality in Siam." See Section B-2.

Siam: Treaties with Foreign Powers, 1920-1927. See Section B-2.

Singh, L. P. "Thai Foreign Policy: The Current Phase." *Asian Survey*, November 1963, pp. 535-543.

A summary of major themes in current Thai foreign policy, with some mention of forces which may affect the future.

Singh, L.P., "The Thai-Cambodian Temple Dispute." *Asian Survey*, October, 1962, pp. 23-26.

A brief statement on a traumatic post-war event in Thai foreign relations — the loss of Kao Phra Wiharn to Cambodia through a decision of the World Court.

Singh, L. P. *The Politics of Economic Cooperation in Asia: A Study of Asian International Organizations*. See Section C-1.

Stanton, Edwin F. *Brief Authority*. New York: Harper & Bros., 1956. 290 pages.

A sympathetic personal account of developments in Thailand, 1946-1953, by a former U.S. ambassador to Thailand.

Stanton, Edwin F. "Spotlight on Thailand." *Foreign Affairs,* October, 1954, pp. 72-85.
  Discusses international forces bearing on Thailand.

Wenk, Klaus. "Die Beziehungen zwischen Deutschland und Thailand," in Jayanama, Wenk, and Biehl, *Thailand.* Hamburg: Das Institut für Asienkunde; Frankfurt and Berlin: Alfred Metzner Verlag, 1960.
  Discusses Thai-German foreign relations.

Wit, Daniel. *Thailand Another Vietnam?* New York: Charles Scribner's Sons, 1968. 205 pages.
  An essayistic sketch of Thai government drawn from secondary sources, with observations on Thai diplomatic and security prospects. No systematic comparisons of Thailand and Vietnam.

Wolf, Charles. *Foreign Aid: Theory and Practice in Southern Asia.* Princeton: Princeton University Press, 1960. 442 pages.
  Includes thirty to forty brief references to specific aspects of foreign aid to Thailand, but provides no extended, systematic treatment of this particular topic.

Young, Kenneth T., Jr. "The Foreign Policies of Thailand." A Paper prepared for the Asia Association and the Association for Asian Studies Conference on the Foreign Policies of Southeast Asian States, May 14-15, 1965. 71 pages.
  An historical account of Thai foreign policy to early 1965. Concludes that, although Thailand's policies will continue to take their cue from the U.S., they will also continue to be distinctively "Thai" in character.

Young, Kenneth T., Jr. *The Southeast Asia Crisis, Background Papers and Proceedings of the Eighth Hammarskjold Forum.* See Section A.

Young, Kenneth T., Jr. "The Special Role of American Advisers in Thailand, 1902-1949." *Asia,* Spring, 1969, pp. 1-31.
  An account, the first to be based on both Thai and American sources, of six of the nine American foreign affairs advisers to the government of Thailand, 1902-1949. Only the first adviser, Edward Stobel, was selected exclusively by the Thais; each of the others was selected by the American incumbent with assistance from Harvard University and the State Department.

D.
THE BUREAUCRACY AND PUBLIC ADMINISTRATION

The intricacies and subtleties of the Thai bureaucracy defy adequate description. The following items deal with aspects of administrative action and the formal structures within which action occurs. But they do not add up to a comprehensive portrait.

Most interesting and broadly informative are the relatively few studies which have an explanatory purpose — i.e., those which attempt to view Thai public administration in its larger social and political context, since the Thai bureaucracy is indeed a significant component of the Thai social system. Mosel's "Thai Administrative Behavior," although published in 1957, remains an incisive statement of the social and psychological factors that make Thai administration what it is. The two most recent extensive studies of this genre are Riggs, *Thailand: The Modernization of a Bureaucratic Polity,* and Siffin, *The Thai Bureaucracy: Institutional Change and Development.*

There are a growing number of descriptive studies and reports on particular aspects of Thai government and administration. Some material of this kind was produced at the Thai Institute of Public Administration, Thammasat University, in the form of Master's theses, many of which are mimeographed. In April, 1966, the IPA became a faculty of the new National Institute of Development Administration (NIDA). NIDA should continue to be a useful source of data on Thai public administration.

A substantial collection of papers and reports has been produced by AID technicians and AID contract personnel, and military activities have also generated studies and data relevant for the study of public administration.

Part one of this section describes aspects of the administrative system generally; parts two and three deal primarily with civil service administration and with revenue and finance administration. Some basic data on Thai public administration will be found in the general survey volumes cited in the first section of this guide and in the sections on political leaders and the political system (C-1), on subnational government (C-5), and on the Thai economy (E-1, 2, 3).

1. The Administrative System

Angsusingha, Pakorn. *The Community Development Program in Thailand.* Bangkok: Department of Public Welfare, Ministry of Interior, 1958. 47 pages.

An official description of the establishment and early phases of community development activities in Thailand. The author was at the time of writing, the Director General of the Public Welfare Department.

Bunnag, Tej. "The Provincial Administration of Siam from 1892 to 1915." Unpublished Ph.D. dissertation, Oxford University, 1968.

Perhaps the definitive study of the formulation and implementation of provincial reform under King Chulalongkorn and Prince Damrong.

Evers, Hans-Dieter. "The Formation of a Social Class Structure: Urbanization, Bureaucratization and Social Mobility in Thailand." See Section G-1.

Evers, Hans-Dieter. "Social Mobility Among Thai Bureaucrats." *Journal of Southeast Asian History,* September, 1966, pp. 110-115.

The basic conclusion of this study is that "in the course of urbanization, social mobility into at least one specific stratum of Thai society [the bureaucratic elite] has declined," and that this is owing largely to occupational specialization, bureaucratization and differential fertility.

Huvanandana, Malai, and William J. Siffin. "Public Administration in Thailand," in S. S. Hsueh (ed.), *Public Administration in South and Southeast Asia.* Brussels: International Institute of Administrative Sciences, 1962, pp. 157-187. (Also issued by the Institute of Public Administration, Thammasat University, Bangkok, n.d. 50 pages, offset.)

A description of the Thai "philosophy" of public administration, development of the Thai bureaucracy, reform of the Thai government, and expansion of the service state in Thailand. Considers the characteristics of authority in the system and relations between politics and administration.

Ibrahim, A. Rashid. "Public Administration in Thailand (A Cursory View of Main Features)." *Thai Journal of Public Administration*, October, 1961, pp. 340-357.

    A description of Thai public administration by the former deputy executive secretary of ECAFE. Concludes that Thai administration compares favorably with other Asian countries.

Jayanama, Direck. "Buddhism and Administration." See Section G-2.

Manual of Organization of the Government of Thailand. Bangkok: Institute of Public Administration, Thammasat University, 1959-1965.

    A series of organization manuals for each of twelve government ministries and the Office of the Prime Minister: public health, agriculture, national development, justice, foreign affairs, economic affairs, communications, industry, interior, finance, education, defense. The manuals were published over a seven-year period and are now out of date.

Mosel, James N. "Thai Administrative Behavior," in W. J. Siffin (ed.), *Toward the Comparative Study of Public Administration*. Bloomington: Indiana University Press, 1959, pp. 278-324.

    A distinguished essay which charts the historical development of the Thai bureaucracy and delineates the socio-cultural context of contemporary Thai public administration.

Mousny, André. *The Economy of Thailand: An Appraisal of a Liberal Exchange Policy*. See Section E-1.

Neher, Clark D. *Development in Rural Thailand*. Los Angeles: Academic Advisory Council for Thailand, University of California at Los Angeles, 1969. 20 pages.

    This paper, presented at a conference on Local Authority in Thailand, examines relations between a northern Thai village and the district level of official government, describes the working of sukhapiban committees in districts within Chiengmai province, and treats other associations briefly — commune committee, farmers' group, and irrigation association. Concludes that there is a significant political element at the village level, and offers a series of recommendations to enhance developmental potentialities in rural Thailand, stressing ways of mobilizing the considerable talents of the political stratum of the rural communities.

Organization and Management of the Ministry of Education: Survey and Recommendations. Bangkok: Bureau of the Budget,

Organization and Management Division, October, 1966. 186 pages + appendices.

A survey of the present formal structure and operation of the Ministry of Education with recommendations for structural change within the Ministry. Basically an "O & M" exercise, which avoids "hard" questions about relationships between educational organization and the social goals of education.

Organizational Directory of the Government of Thailand. See Section I-3.

Parker, Glen L. *Accelerating the Rate of Economic Growth: A Study in Economic Policy.* See Section E-3.

Parker, Glen L. *The Industrial Development of Thailand: A Summary of Recommendations.* See Section E-3.

Program for Strengthening Public Administration in the Kingdom of Thailand. Bangkok and Chicago: Public Administration Service, May, 1952. 31 pages.

The report of a preliminary survey examining budget and accounting procedures, the tax system, and the relationship between central planning agencies and municipal administrative organizations. Offers proposals to strengthen public institutions and procedures in Thailand. Interesting as a bench mark.

Reeve, W. D. *Public Administration in Siam.* London: Royal Institute of International Affairs, 1951. 93 pages.

A description of the Thai administrative system following establishment of the limited monarchy in 1932, written by a former customs advisor to the Thai government. The concluding chapter discusses merits and defects of the system.

Riggs, Fred W. *The Ecology of Public Administration.* Bombay and London: Asia Publishing House, 1961. 152 pages.

A collection of three lectures delivered at the Indian Institute of Public Administration, on the ecology of administration in the United States, Thailand, and the Philippines. Chapter Two deals with the ecology of administration in traditional Thailand and Chapter Three with internal and external factors affecting change in Thailand and the Philippines.

Riggs, Fred W. *Thailand: The Modernization of a Bureaucratic Polity.* See Section C-1.

Semthiti, Theb. "Department of Administrative Inspection." Unpublished Master's thesis. Bangkok: Institute of Public Administration, Thammasat University, 1959. 158 pages.

Describes the organization and functions of a department which served as an important bureaucratic surveillance and control mechanism during the Pibul regime. The department reflected one approach to the control of administrative behavior in the Thai Bureaucracy.

Shor, Edgar L. "The Public Service," in Joseph L. Sutton (ed.), *Problems of Politics and Administration in Thailand.* Bloomington: Institute of Training for Public Service, Indiana University, 1962, pp. 32-40.

A partly descriptive, partly analytical essay on the Thai bureaucracy, with emphasis on the civil service system.

Shor, Edgar L. "The Thai Bureaucracy." *Administrative Science Quarterly,* June, 1960, pp. 66-86.

Relates the distinctive characteristics of the Thai bureaucracy to its socio-political milieu. Focuses on institutional patterns and modes of behavior of career officialdom. Data obtained through interviews with representative officials and from records in the ministries and the Thai Civil Service Commission.

Siffin, William J. "The Development of the Office of the President of the Council of Ministers, B.E. 2502-3." *Thai Journal of Public Administration,* October, 1960, pp. 80-106.

Discusses developments in the formal structure of the office of the Prime Minister under Marshal Sarit following the revolution of October, 1958.

Siffin, William J. *The Thai Bureaucracy: Institutional Change and Development* Honolulu: East-West Center Press, 1966. 300 pages.

Traces the development of the contemporary Thai bureaucratic system. Describes the traditional bureaucracy, analyzes the reformation of the late nineteenth century and the developments of the post-reformation period. Characterizes the present bureaucracy in terms of its general normative structure as a social substructure.

Silcock, T. H. "Promotion of Industry and the Planning Process." See Section E-3.

Suvanajata, Titaya. *Perceived Leader Role of Community Development Workers in Thailand.* Bangkok: U.S. Agency for International Development, 1964. 78 pages.

An analysis of the leadership functions of community development workers, based on a questionnaire survey of 102 workers. Some interesting information on the role-perceptions of CD workers.

Thomas, M. Ladd. "Political Socialization of the Thai-Islam." See Section G-4.

Thomas, M. Ladd. "Thai Public Administration." *New Zealand Journal of Public Administration,* September, 1962, pp. 3-33.

A broad description of the Thai administrative system, which goes beyond the formal structural characteristics to take account of certain ecological factors that help explain the workings of the bureaucracy.

Utthangkorn, Amphorn. "Bus Regulation in the Bangkok-Thonburi Metropolitan Area." Unpublished Master's thesis. Bangkok: Institute of Public Administration, Thammasat University, 1960. 189 pages.

A careful and extensive description of actual patterns of regulatory administration found in this field as of the late 1950's.

Vilaichitt, Snit. *Kamnan and Puyaiban: Their Origin, History and Importance to Village Dévelopment in Thailand.* Bangkok: U.S. Agency for International Development, 1967.

A translation of a 1964 work by the Thai Deputy Director General of the Department of Local Administration, Ministry of Interior. While this is one of the few works in English which describe the formal roles of kamnan-puyaiban, tracing their development from the reforms of King Chulalongkorn, its major value lies in showing the thinking of a high Thai official about bringing village actualities more into accord with the ideal conceived by government administrators. The translation is poor.

Wales, H. G. Quaritch. *Ancient Siamese Government and Administration.* See Section B-1.

Yatsushiro, Toshio. *The Village Organizer in Thailand: A Study of His Needs and Problems.* Bangkok: U.S. Agency for International Development, 1964. 107 pages.

A study of village organizers of the Department of Community Development, Ministry of Interior. Suggests, for example, that village organizers should be male, older than 25 years, have rural backgrounds, and should concentrate on fostering local leadership.

2. Personnel and Civil Service

Choosanay, Manoo. "The Role of Discipline in Administration of the Department of Interior, Thailand." Unpublished Master's thesis. Bangkok: Institute of Public Administration, Thammasat University, 1960. 93 pages.

    A description of formal penalties and informal procedures in the Department of Interior, by an experienced Thai government official. Interesting for its personal observations.

Gaewchaiyo, Ura. "The Development of Thai Civil Service Commission." Unpublished Master's thesis. Bangkok: Institute of Public Administration, Thammasat University, 1959. 138 pages.

    A description of the development of the Thai civil service system, containing detailed information about Thai civil service law and policy. Also, an extensive description of the structure of the Thai Civil Service Commission as of 1959.

Hansakul, Chakra. "A Study of Pay Policy and Administration in the Thai Civil Service." Unpublished Master's thesis. Bangkok: Institute of Public Administration, Thammasat University, 1959. 228 pages.

    An extensive description of past and present pay policy and administration in Thai civil service. Some figures on pay scales. Considerable information on some aspects of bureaucratic modernization.

Marsh, Harry W., and Ernest J. Barbour. *Public Personnel Management in Thailand.* Bangkok: U.S. Agency for International Development, 1961. 20 pages.

    A brief survey of Thai personnel practices. Stresses the need for a system of position classifications as opposed to the "personal rank" system now in use in the Thai civil service, but concludes that needed reforms are not yet likely to occur.

Shor, Edgar L. "The Public Service." See Section D-1.

Siffin, William J. "The Civil Service System of the Kingdom of Thailand." *International Review of Administrative Services,* March, 1960, pp. 255-268.

    A brief history and description of the Thai civil service system.

Siffin, William J. "Personnel Processes of the Thai Bureaucracy," in Ferrel Heady and Sybil Stokes (eds.), *Papers in Comparative Administration*. Ann Arbor: Institute of Public Administration, University of Michigan, 1962, pp. 207-228.

A systematic description of basic processes characteristic of the Thai bureaucracy: procurement of personnel resources, the ways in which they are ordered or organized, and the techniques of energizing or motivating personnel.

Soonthornsima, Chinnawoot. "The Relation of College Education and Pay Levels in the Thai Civil Service." Unpublished Master's thesis. Bangkok: Institute of Public Administration, Thammasat University, 1959. 149 pages.

A historical description of the civil service pay system. Examines pay scales and analyzes the relationship between pay levels and higher education as of the late 1950's.

Sukhum Nayapradit, Luang. "The Civil Service System." *Thai Journal of Public Administration*, January, 1964, pp. 437-449.

An outline of the organization and legal provisions of the Thai civil service system by the then-director general of the Thai Civil Service Commission.

Suwanagul, Kasem. "Recruitment and Promotion in the Thai Civil Service." *Thai Journal of Public Administration*, October, 1963, pp. 340-357.

A critical essay on recruitment and promotion in the Thai Civil Service drawn from the author's doctoral dissertation. Concludes that the system's prevailing philosophy cannot meet future personnel needs.

Udyanin, Kasem, and Rufus D. Smith. *The Public Service in Thailand: Organization, Recruitment and Training*. Brussels: International Institute of Administrative Sciences, 1954. 64 pages.

A general description of the traditional and contemporary formal structures of the Thai public service. Brief discussion of the Civil Service Act of 1952.

3. Revenue and Finance Administration

Amatayakul, Ravi, and Shrikrishna A. Pandit. "Financial Institutions in Thailand." See Section E-1.

The Bureaucracy and Public Administration

Final Report, Project for Modernization of Government Fiscal Management. Bangkok and Chicago: Public Administration Service, 1963. 86 pages.

    The final report of the PAS contract team on modernization of Thai fiscal administration. Contains sections on budget preparation, accounting and fiscal reporting, auditing, revenue administration. (In Thai and English.)

Loftus, John A. "Problems of Fiscal Management." See Section E-1.

Neher, Clark D. "District Level Politics in Thailand." See Section C-5.

A Public Development Program for Thailand. See Section E-3.

Report on Organization and Administration of the Revenue Department, Kingdom of Thailand. Bangkok and Chicago: Public Administration Service, Report No. M-11, March, 1963. 76 pages.

    A study of the organization and administration of the Revenue Department with recommendations for improvement.

Revenue Laws and Their Administration. See Section C-3.

Silabhundhu, Charoensook. "Study of National Control of Sukaphiban Finance." See Section C-5.

Sommers, William A. *Statistics on Municipal Revenues in Thailand, 1963 to 1966.* See Section C-5.

Sommers, William A. *A Summary of the Budget Process for the Changwad Local Government.* Bangkok: U.S. Agency for International Development, September, 1967. 17 pages.

    Prepared in cooperation with the Thai Department of Local Administration, this is a brief, useful description of local government budgets with extensive tabular data on local government incomes and expenditures.

Wimoniti, Wira. "Historical Patterns of Tax Administration in Thailand." Unpublished Master's thesis. Bangkok: Institute of Public Administration, Thammasat University, 1961. 184 pages.

    An extensive historical description of Thai revenue administration. Includes a substantial amount of information on practices and problems during the 1950's.

E.
THE THAI ECONOMY AND ECONOMIC DEVELOPMENT

The economy of Thailand is in the midst of rapid and extensive changes. But the processes of change are not entirely new, and the economy itself is a complex mix of private-enterprise traders and agricultural smallholders plus direct public economic activity.

Governmental involvement in economic matters is substantial, varied, and growing. A considerable part of this effort has been devoted to the development of the economic infrastructure. Another major concern has been the protection and expansion of Thailand's position in an international economic setting. (The rapid expansion of Thai maize exports to Japan is one of the few export "success stories" in Southeast Asia.) As of now, Thailand's economic situation appears good, owing to enlightened development policy and fortuitous events, such as the Vietnam war and the decline of Burma as a leading rice exporter. However, the limitations inherent in small, primary exporting economies make the long-run economic outlook for Thailand problematic, as does its very high population growth rate. Some form of effective regional cooperation, and/or major trade or tariff concessions by the industrial powers, would seem to be essential for long-run economic success.

The expanding scope of Thai economic concerns is reflected in a blossoming literature. Yet the points of departure for Thai economic studies are relatively few. Ingram's bench mark study of *Economic Change in Thailand Since 1850* surveys a hundred years of shifting, expanding economic activity to 1950. The report of the World Bank (International Bank for Reconstruction and Development), *A Public Development Program for Thailand*, describes general characteristics of the economy as of the latter 1950's. Mousny's *The Economy of Thailand* analyzes a most significant feature of the Thai economy — the exchange policy, which has had profound effects upon economic activity. Muscat's *Development Strategy in Thailand* examines a broad array of developmental needs, problems, and opportunities. And one of the best statements of recent economic developments in Thailand is T. H. Silcock's "Outline of Economic Development, 1945-1965," the lead essay in his *Thailand: Social and Economic Studies in Development*.

This brings us to a substantial number of specialized studies, cited in parts one to three in this section, which are concerned with economic processes and institutions. In addition, economic information will be found in the survey publications cited in Sections A, D, and G.

The first part of this section covers the literature on aspects of the general economy; the second deals with foreign trade, particularly the rice trade; the third concentrates on planning and economic development; and the fourth cites various sources of statistical information. The sources of statistical information about Thailand are many and varied, including government departments and banks, United Nations agencies, private banks, the U.S. aid mission to Thailand. Many of these data sources are unreliable and therefore must be used with caution. For reliability, regularity of publication, and scope of coverage, the best sources are the monthly and annual reports of the Bank of Thailand. The quarterly *Bulletin of Statistics* of the National Statistical Office, the *Economic Survey of Asia and the Far East* published annually by ECAFE, and the numerous reports of the National Economic Development Board are also sources that are cited here. Specialized agencies of the United Nations, such as the FAO, the WHO, and UNESCO, report various kinds of economic information too.

1. The Economy

Amatayakul, Ravi, and Shrikrishna A. Pandit. "Financial Institutions in Thailand." *International Monetary Fund Staff Papers*, Vol. VII, 1960-61, pp. 464-489.

Describes the principal formal financial institutions of Thailand: the Bank of Thailand (the central bank), twenty-seven commercial banks, the Government Savings Bank, the Industrial Finance Corporation, credit cooperatives, and insurance companies.

Andrews, James M. *Siam: Second Rural Economic Survey, 1934-1935*. Bangkok: Bangkok Times Press, 1936. 396 pages.

A sample survey conducted under the direction of a Harvard University anthropologist. Together with the first rural economic survey (see Zimmerman, below), this report provides data on income, expenditure, investment, and credit in rural Thailand as of the time of the study. Useful historical bench mark.

Artamonoff, George L. *State Owned Enterprises in Thailand*. Bangkok: U.S. Agency for International Development, 1965. 212 pages.

A compilation of financial and production data on about one hundred state-owned enterprises, based largely on information drawn from the Thai government budget office. This study covers perhaps a third of the existing state-owned enterprises, according to "informed guesses," and contains two or three pages of descriptive information about each. Includes recommendations for retention or disposition of individual enterprises, essentially based upon economic premises.

Ayal, Eliezer B. "Public Policies in Thailand Under the Constitutional Regime: A Case Study of an Underdeveloped Country." See Section C-1.

Basic Information Concerning Investment in Thailand. Bangkok: Board of Investment, n.d. Issued about 1960; reissued irregularly.

Information for prospective foreign investors in industrial enterprises in Thailand. Includes some economic data, and sets forth official policy toward foreign investment.

Behrman, Jere R. "Price Elasticity of the Marketed Surplus of a Subsistence Crop." *Journal of Farm Economics*, November, 1966, pp. 875-893.

Applies the model developed in the author's book, cited below, to the case of Thai rice. Some new nonlinear estimates of the total supply response of Thai rice are also presented.

Behrman, Jere R. *Supply Response in Underdeveloped Agriculture: A Case Study of Four Major Annual Crops in Thailand, 1937-1963*. Amsterdam: North-Holland Publishing Company, 1968. 446 pages.

This excellent empirical study develops a model of the Nerlovian type for the supply response in underdeveloped agriculture. The total supply response model is then applied to

Thailand's four annual crops — rice, cassava, corn, and kenaf. Data employed is at the changwad level of aggregation; the marketed supply model is applied only in the case of rice, using nationally aggregated data. The estimates obtained suggest that Thai farmers "respond significantly and substantially" to variables influencing income and risk. The response to price changes was found to be remarkable. Includes an extensive bibliography.

Biriyayodhin, Parayut. "The Management of Government Enterprises Under the Control of the Ministry of Industry." Unpublished Master's thesis. Bangkok: Institute of Public Administration, Thammasat University, 1961. 125 pages.

Describes the organization of the Ministry of Industry and its administration of a group of public enterprises in terms of formal structure and operations. Also discusses briefly the background of public enterprises in Thailand.

Board of Trade Directory, 1967. Bangkok: Board of Trade of Thailand.

Arranged in nine sections, each containing about ten to one hundred forty pages: general information on trade, taxation, the economy; chambers of commerce, commercial banks, trade associations; membership directory, Thai Board of Trade (about four hundred firms); exportable products with key to firms handling them; diplomatic, consular, and trade representatives; government organization; legislation affecting trade; airlines, shipping companies, Bangkok hotels. (Available from Board of Trade, 150 Rajbopit Road, Bangkok.)

Economic Survey of Asia and the Far East. See Section E-4.

Fourth Annual Compendium of Assistance to Thailand. See Section C-6.

Freyn, Hubert. "Culture and Economics in Thailand." See Section G-1.

Golay, Frank H., Ralph Anspach, M. Ruth Pfanner, and Eliezer B. Ayal. *Underdevelopment and Economic Nationalism in Southeast Asia.* See Section A.

Gorden, W. M. "The Exchange Rate System and the Taxation of Trade," in T. H. Silcock (ed.), *Thailand: Social and Economic Studies in Development.* Canberra: Australian National University Press, 1967, pp. 151-169.

Describes the Thai multiple exchange rate system, which

operated up to 1955, and taxes and controls on trade since 1955. On the multiple exchange rate system see also Ingram, Mousny, and Yand, cited below.

Hughes, Rufus B., *et al*. *Thailand Agricultural Cooperatives: An Evaluation with Recommendations for Improvement.* Bangkok: U.S. Agency for International Development, 1968. 140 pages.

A sharp, informed criticism of the fifty-year-old cooperative movement in Thailand — or actually, of the quasi-cooperative movement, since Thai cooperatives are dominated, in management, operation, and finance, by one or more government ministries.

Ingram, James C. *Economic Change in Thailand Since 1850.* Stanford: Stanford University Press, 1955. 254 pages.

A definitive study of Thai economic history, which traces the economic impact of the West, beginning in the middle of the nineteenth century, and provides a valuable perspective for studying the contemporary Thai economy.

Isaraphundh, Glom. "A Comparison of the Legal-Economic Features of Cooperative Organization in the U.S. and Thailand." Unpublished Ph.D. dissertation, University of Wisconsin, 1961. 308 pages.

Describes development, organization, and operations of Thai cooperative associations. The study is essentially concerned with institutional characteristics.

Janlekha, Kamol Odd. *A Study of the Economy of a Rice-Growing Village in Central Thailand.* Bangkok: Ministry of Agriculture, 1955. 199 pages.

A reprint of the author's doctoral dissertation, submitted to Cornell University in 1955. A careful ordering of economic data collected in the Cornell study of the Thai village of Bang Chan, in Phranakorn Province. Provides substantial insight into the economic facets of life in a central Thai village.

Jittemana, Phimal. "Agriculture in a Developing Economy: A Mid-Century Appraisal of Thailand's Agriculture." Unpublished Ph.D. dissertation, University of Wisconsin, 1959. 256 pages.

Describes basic features and problems of the agricultural sector and its place in the total economic process of Thailand. Also deals briefly with the social features of agriculture, including the role of the *wat* in village life, rural schools and education, and the social status of the Thai peasant.

Judd, Lawrence C. *Dry Rice Agriculture in Northern Thailand.* Ithaca: Cornell University, Southeast Asia Program, Data Paper No. 52, 1964. 72 pages + appendices.

Derived from the author's doctoral dissertation for Cornell University (1961), entitled "Chao Rai: Dry Rice Farming in Northern Thailand." A detailed study of "swidden farming" (shifting agriculture) in the Baw district of Nam province in Northern Thailand from January, 1958, to May, 1959. Subjects covered by the study include district soil and plant resources, technology, occupations, and economy.

Keesing, Donald B. "Thailand and Malaysia: A Case for a Common Market?" *Malayan Economic Review,* October, 1965, pp. 102-113.

Suggests that in Southeast Asia the most economically promising common market bets are Thailand and Malaysia.

Keyfitz, Nathan. "Political-Economic Aspects of Urbanization in South and Southeast Asia." See Section C-5.

Krisanamis, Phairach. "Paddy Price Movements and Their Effect on the Economic Situation of Farmers in the Central Plain of Thailand." Unpublished Ph.D. dissertation, Indiana University, 1967. 203 pages.

A study of the patterns of price movements of paddy (rough rice) in central Thailand. Also examines the relation between paddy price changes and agricultural income.

Lee, S. Y. "Currency, Banking and Foreign Exchange of Thailand." *Far Eastern Economic Review,* November 24, December 1, and December 8, 1960.

A useful descriptive survey of the Thai fiscal system as of 1960, spread over three consecutive issues.

Loftus, John A. "Problems of Fiscal Management." *Thai Journal of Public Administration,* July, 1961, pp. 136-150.

A frank and authoritative statement by a former economic advisor to the Government of Thailand on problems of budget and debt management. Also discusses the need for improvement of the commercial banking system and related financial institutions.

Loftus, John A. *Reports of the Economic Advisor to the Government of Thailand.* Bangkok: Ministry of Finance, 1956-1962. Unpublished.

Thirteen semiannual reports, in memorandum form, on various aspects of the Thai economy and governmental economic affairs. These reports were not prepared for extensive circulation, but as working documents they are useful sources of information on real problems of political economy — economic planning, problems of tax administration, state enterprises, and governmental organization for the administration of economic affairs — in Thailand during the period covered.

Long, Millard F., et al. *Economic and Social Conditions Among Farmers in Changwad Khonkaen.* Bangkok: U.S. Agency for International Development, 1964. 164 pages.

A general description of an important Northeast province, including resources, production, income and wealth, demography and mobility, government services, and social behavior. Numerous tables, maps, and graphs.

Moerman, Michael. *Agricultural Change and Peasant Choice in a Thai Village.* Berkeley: University of California Press, 1968. 227 pages.

Applies an ethnoscience perspective to a major native institution, rice farming, in order to analyze the rationality of peasant production decisions, and argues that any agency wishing to alter those decisions must first understand their rationale. Perhaps the most detailed anthropological account of Thai wet rice farming available in English, and the first book-length study of the Thai-Lue. The village studied, Ban Ping, is in Chiengrai province in northern Thailand. A revision of the author's Ph.D. dissertation, "Farming in Ban Phaed: Technological Decisions and Their Consequences for the External Relations of a Thai-Lue Village," Yale University, 1964.

Moerman, Michael. "Western Culture and the Thai Way of Life." See Section G-1.

Motooka, Takeshi. "Problems of Land Reform in Thailand with Reference to the Japanese Experience." *Japan's Future in Southeast Asia,* Symposium Series II, The Center for Southeast Asian Studies, Kyoto University, July, 1966, pp. 15-28.

Challenges the widespread notion that Thailand is one of the few developing countries without a land tenancy problem. The percentage of farmers who pay some form of rent in the Central Plain (Thailand's rice bowl) is high and rising, as land values increase and farm enterprise patterns shift from extensive toward intensive farming. (See also Yano, this section.)

Mousny, André. *The Economy of Thailand: An Appraisal of a*

Liberal Exchange Policy. Bangkok: Social Sciences Association Press of Thailand, 1964. 278 pages.

An informative description and analysis of the contemporary Thai economy, including the wartime exchange controls, the multiple-rate exchange system used for several years after the war, and the liberal exchange policy which replaced the multiple rate system. Provides information on industrial development in Thailand through 1961, and seeks to show that continued development is linked with the existing exchange policy. A relatively technical study.

Myint, Hla. "The Inward and Outward Looking Countries of Southeast Asia and the Economic Future of the Region." *Japan's Future in Southeast Asia,* Symposium Series II, The Center for Southeast Asian Studies, Kyoto University, July, 1966, pp. 1-14.

Argues that the basic economic problem of Southeast Asian countries concerns a more effective and complete use of relatively abundant resources. To attain this environment, they should adopt an outward-looking development policy (as opposed to an inward-looking or autarchic policy permitted by the huge internal markets of India and China), making full use of international trade opportunities and regional cooperation. To date, only Thailand, Malaysia, and the Philippines (in the region) have followed such a policy. An excellent nontechnical introduction to regional economic development problems.

Myrdal, Gunnar. *Asian Drama: An Inquiry Into the Poverty of Nations.* 3 vols. New York: Random House, 1968. 2,284 pages.

Pertains most directly to India and Southern Asia, but has some general relevance to Thailand, although not as a prime source. Volume I is essentially a political history. Part three of Volume I and all of Volume II are detailed economic and demographic analyses of South and Southeast Asia. Volume III consists largely of appendices in which particular problems are discussed.

Paauw, Douglas S. "Economic Progress in Southeast Asia." *Journal of Asian Studies,* November, 1963, pp. 69-92.

Examines differences in the economic performance of Southeast Asian countries in terms of restoring and surpassing their pre-World War II levels of output, and in terms of key variables in the process of economic growth. Useful, well-documented study.

Panitpakdi, Prot. "National Accounts Estimates of Thailand," in

T. H. Silcock (ed.), *Thailand Social and Economic Studies in Development.* Canberra: Australian National University Press, 1967, pp. 105-127.

A brief analysis of official Thai national accounts estimates, focusing on the structures of national production, consumption, and capital formation, and changes in these structures over the five-year period 1958-1963.

Pfanner, David E., and Jasper Ingersoll. "Theravada Buddhism and Village Economic Behavior, A Burmese and Thai Comparison." See Section G-2.

Platenius, Hans. *The Northeast of Thailand: Its Problems and Potentialities.* Bangkok: National Economic Development Board, October, 1963. 132 pages.

Describes in some detail the economy of Northeast Thailand, including the economic infrastructure. Suggests planning methods which are suitable to the Northeast and concludes that first priority in economic planning must be given to needs expressed by the villagers themselves.

Rozental, Alek A. "Branch Banking in Thailand." *The Journal of Developing Areas,* October, 1968, pp. 37-50.

Concludes that Thailand has a highly developed network of private institutions — at least five hundred — providing general banking facilities outside the capital. Contains hard-to-obtain data on the number and location of commercial banks in the kingdom, their demand and time deposits, and loans and overdrafts. Interesting for the demonstrated connection between the Thai commercial banking system and political power.

Rozental, Alek A. *Finance and Development in Thailand.* New York: Praeger, 1970. 386 pages.

Definitive study of Thai financial institutions, including sources of finance for private enterprise. Describes and analyzes the relevant institutions, evaluates their performance, and suggests reforms. Contributes significant insights into the politics of Thai banking and finance.

Silcock, T. H. *The Economic Development of Thai Agriculture.* Ithaca: Cornell University Press, 1970. 250 pages.

A work of fundamental importance. Careful and informative analysis of agricultural development in Thailand, and a discerning case study of the effects of public policy and Thai developmental efforts upon the rural sector. Most of the data are from the mid-1960's, and the work lays a foundation for useful longitudinal analysis. This work supplements and extends the more limited treatment of agriculture in Silcock, ed., *Thailand: Social and Economic Studies in Development.*

Silcock, T. H. "Money and Banking," in T. H. Silcock (ed.), *Thailand: Social and Economic Studies in Development.* Canberra: Australian National University Press, 1967, pp. 171-205.

An overview of the Thai banking system from the Chulalongkorn era to the present. Good description and analysis of the role of the Bank of Thailand and of the Thai, Chinese, and Western commercial banks in contemporary Thai politics.

Silcock, T. H. "The Rice Premium and Agricultural Diversification," in T. H. Silcock (ed.), *Thailand: Social and Economic Studies in Development.* Canberra: Australian National University Press, 1967, pp. 231-257.

A well-reasoned analysis concluding that the rice premium (the tax on rice exports) has, for the most part, been economically beneficial. It has encouraged agricultural diversification; and it has made it possible, by keeping wages and the domestic cost of living down, for Thailand to maintain relatively tax-free exports, while promoting import-substituting industrialization. For a somewhat contrary view, see Usher, Section E-2.

Silcock, T. H. (ed.). *Thailand: Social and Economic Studies in Development.* Canberra: Australian National University Press, in association with Duke University Press, Durham, N.C., 1967. 334 pages.

A thoughtful and perceptive reader, concerned mostly with aspects of the Thai economy, including development problems and prospects, but also containing several significant statements on aspects of Thai society. (Most of the chapters also are cited individually in this bibliography.)

Sithi-Amnuai, Paul. "The Economy of Southern Thailand." *Far Eastern Economic Review,* October 25, 1962, pp. 237-243.

A brief sketch of socio-economic characteristics of Southern Thailand, noting the importance to Thailand of the development of this Islamic, Malay-speaking area, which is both minerally and agriculturally rich. Government developmental activities in the area are summarized.

Sithi-Amnuai, Paul (ed.). *Finance and Banking in Thailand: A Study of the Commercial System, 1888-1963.* Bangkok: Thai Watana Panich, 1964. 224 pages.

Traces development of the Thai financial and banking system from its nineteenth-century beginnings, through the Japanese occupation, to present organizational forms. Discusses the problems of the banking system, its institutional changes and activities. Includes a bibliography on banking, finance, and economic development in Thailand.

Sithi-Amnuai, Paul. "Thai Power Industry." *Far Eastern Economic Review*, May 10, 1962, pp. 282-287.

A description of the electric energy facilities of Thailand, which are being rapidly and extensively developed.

Thisyamondol, Pantum, Virach Arromdee, and Millard F. Long. *Agricultural Credit in Thailand: Theory, Data, Policy*. Bangkok: Faculty of Economics and Business Administration, Kasetsart University, 1965. 70 pages.

Concludes that the vast majority of Thai farmers are not "problem debtors." Debts are heavy only among commercial farmers of the Central Plain — those with relatively large incomes. Large debts are infrequent among the semi-subsistence farmers of the Northeast and other regions of the country, not primarily because credit is unavailable but because they do not wish to borrow. The study is based on a sample of 742 farms in forty-one provinces.

Usher, Dan. "Income as a Measure of Productivity: Alternative Comparisons of Agricultural and Non-Agricultural Productivity in Thailand." *Economica*, November, 1966, pp. 430-441.

Argues that the usual sectoral productivity measure, based on the ratio of the sector's income share in national income accounts to the labor force employed in the sector, does not accurately represent productivity. By making various corrections in the Thai data for 1963, the author estimates that the ratio of farm to nonfarm income per worker should be increased from about 1:10 to 1:3.

Usher, Dan. "Thai Interest Rates." *The Journal of Development Studies*, April, 1967, pp. 267-279.

Two questions about interest rates in underdeveloped countries are examined, using data from Thailand by way of example: (1) what is the relation between rates of interest charged on loans and rates of return on productive investments? (2) to what extent are village interest rates linked with urban and international interest rates?

Van Roy, Edward. "Economic Dualism and Economic Change Among the Hill Tribes of Thailand." See Section G-4.

Van Roy, Edward. "An Interpretation of the Northern Thai Peasant Economy." *Journal of Asian Studies*, May, 1967, pp. 421-432.

Examines *miang* production and consumption as a microcosmic reflection of the Northern Thai peasant economy. Notes the persistence of traditional patterns of economic behavior, which operate in accord with the hierarchical concept of status and rank.

Wijeyewardene, Gehan. "A Note on Irrigation and Agriculture in a North Thai Village." See Section G-1.

Yang, Shu-Chin. *A Multiple Exchange Rate System: An Appraisal of Thailand's Experience, 1946-1955.* Madison: University of Wisconsin Press, 1957. 200 pages.

This study of Thailand's economic control system in the years after World War II includes a summary description of the Thai economy, an economic history of the wartime and early post-war years, and a technical analysis of the Thai government's foreign exchange control efforts. Amounts to a case in Thai public policy as well as an economic analysis.

Yano, Toru. "Land Tenure in Thailand." *Asian Survey*, October, 1968, pp. 853-863.

Questions the widely held belief that the Thai farmer is, in the great majority of cases, an owner-cultivator and that Thailand has no serious land problem. Yano's study indicates that Thailand has two major land problems — fragmentation and customary land possession outside the scope of the land law. (See also Motooka, this section.)

Zimmerman, Carl C. *Siam: Rural Economic Survey, 1930-1931.* Bangkok: Bangkok Times Press, 1931. 321 pages.

The first of two rural economic surveys conducted in the 1930's. Along with the later work by Andrews, this benchmark study is a useful point of reference for studying certain patterns of change in the economy of rural Thailand.

2. Foreign Trade

Ayal, Eliezer B. "The Impact of Export Taxes on the Domestic Economy of Underdeveloped Countries." *The Journal of Development Studies*, July, 1965, pp. 330-362.

Compares the domestic economic effect of the Thai rice premium and the Burmese Agricultural Marketing Board tax on rice, including their impact on agricultural diversification, balance of payments and terms of trade, the urban sector, and factor and resource transfers. Concludes that, while in the case of Thailand a large part of the export tax on rice is shifted backward, both the Thai and Burmese taxes have a wholesome effect on development by encouraging diversification and resource reallocation.

Gorden, W. M. "The Exchange Rate System and the Taxation of Trade." See Section E-1.

Gorden, W. M., and H. V. Richter. "Trade and the Balance of Payments," in T. H. Silcock (ed.), *Thailand: Social and Economic Studies in Development*. Canberra: Australian National University Press, 1967, pp. 128-150.

Describes Thai export trends and prospects, changes in the import patterns, the inflow of foreign capital and aid, and the balance of payments situation, and concludes that Thailand's economic problems are not, at present, principally trade or balance of payments problems.

Ingram, James C. "Thailand's Rice Trade and the Allocation of Resources," in C. D. Cowan (ed.), *The Economic Development of Southeast Asia: Studies in Economic History and Political Economy*. London: George Allen and Unwin, 1964.

A description of Thailand's rice trade, plus a study of the development of the ethnic division of Thai labor — i.e., why the Chinese did not become rice farmers or the Thais wage-laborers in the nineteenth century.

Inthachat, Vichien. "Rice Premium and Its Administration." Unpublished Master's thesis. Bangkok: Institute of Public Administration, Thammasat University, 1960. 98 pages.

Describes the administrative organization of the rice premium program. Includes statistics on rice production, export prices, and the disposition of funds received from rice sales; also identifies companies selling rice under the rice premium program. Good description of the formal aspects of a significant economic activity of Thai government in the post-war period.

Ramakomud, Sriprinya. "Thailand's Foreign Trade: Structure

and Policies, 1951-1960." Unpublished Ph.D. dissertation, Indiana University, 1963. 297 pages.

Examines the consequences of three assertedly important factors affecting Thai foreign trade: (1) import trends; (2) ecological factors affecting domestic productivity; and (3) output inelasticity.

Silcock, T. H. "The Rice Premium and Agricultural Diversification." See Section E-1.

Singh, L. P. *The Politics of Economic Cooperation in Asia: A Study of Asian International Organizations.* See Section C-1.

Sitton, Gordon R., Chaiyond Chuchart, and Bimbandha S. Na Ayudhaya. *The Growing Importance of Upland Crops in the Foreign Trade of Thailand.* Bangkok: Kasetsart University, 1962. 115 pages.

Data on production, export, and import of sixteen upland crops. Changes in resource availability, consumer demands, and industrial needs are discussed in relationship to land use. (In Thai and English.)

Unakul, Snoh. "International Trade and Economic Development of Thailand." Unpublished Ph.D. dissertation, Columbia University, 1962. 320 pages.

The reversal of Thailand's trade patterns (export surpluses to import surpluses) is shown to reflect two related post-war developments: (1) basic changes in government policy, and (2) basic changes in the rate and pattern of post-war economic development within the Thai economy.

Usher, Dan. "The Thai Rice Trade," in T. H. Silcock (ed.), *Thailand: Social and Economic Studies in Development.* Canberra: Australian National University Press, 1967, pp. 207-230.

An informative description of the Thai domestic and export rice trade (production, milling, and marketing), based on extensive field research. Usher concludes that: (1) contrary to popular mythology, the total distribution ("middleman") cost of retailing rice in Thailand is low by European or American standards; and (2) the abolition of the controversial export tax on rice would benefit the farmer rather than increase monopoly profits. For a somewhat contrary view with respect to the development value of the rice premium, see Silcock, "The Rice Premium and Agricultural Diversification," Section E-1.

3. Planning and Economic Development

Atthakor, Bunchana. *Thailand's Economic Development, 1950-1960.* Bangkok: National Economic Development Board, n.d. 51 pages.

A brief summary and review of economic developments, written by a member of the Thai cabinet. Twenty-one pages in English; the remainder in Thai.

Ayal, Eliezer B. "Private Enterprise and Economic Progress in Thailand." *Journal of Asian Studies,* November, 1966, pp. 5-14.

Cautions against "jumping to conclusions" because free enterprise systems, at least in Southeast Asia, have experienced higher rates of growth in recent years than centrally planned ones. Argues that differences between nations in such factors as the availability of entrepreneurs is at least as important as differences in the extent of central planning and government involvement.

Ayal, Eliezer B. "Some Crucial Issues in Thailand's Economic Development." *Pacific Affairs,* Summer, 1961, pp. 157-164.

A sharp criticism of some of the recommendations of the World Bank report, *A Public Development Program for Thailand,* and an argument that economic development will require abandoning emphasis upon a rice economy and using modern production methods in a vigorous campaign of modernization.

Ayal, Eliezer B. "Thailand's Six-Year National Economic Development Plan." *Asian Survey,* January, 1962, pp. 33-43.

Outlines the official developmental plan for 1961-1966 and assesses prospects for future development in Thailand along the lines contemplated in the plan.

Ayal, Eliezer B. "Value Systems and Economic Development in Japan and Thailand." *Journal of Social Issues,* January, 1963, pp. 44-51.

Argues that certain characteristics of Thai society are substantially inconsistent with the development of entrepreneurship among Thais, at least in a manner comparable to the experience in Japan. An implicitly pessimistic essay about prospects for rapid and extensive economic development in Thailand.

Behrman, Jere R. "Significance of Intracountry Variations for

Asian Agricultural Prospects: Central and Northeastern Thailand." *Asian Survey*, March, 1968, pp. 157-173.

Examines variations in agricultural productivity (using rice production as the main indicator) across the provinces of Central and Northeastern Thailand.

Bell, Peter. "The Role of the Entrepreneur in Economic Development: A Case Study in Thailand." Unpublished Ph.D. dissertation, University of Wisconsin, 1967.

An attempt to develop a theory of entrepreneurship that permits the identification of entrepreneurs and predicts the circumstances of their emergence. Based on a sample survey of some eighty Thai entrepreneurs in the modern manufacturing sector, all of whom had received special promotional privileges, this study examines the factors most affecting their decisions to enter business.

Brown, L. R. *Agricultural Diversification and Economic Development in Thailand: A Case Study*. Washington, D.C.: U.S. Department of Agriculture, Economic Research Division, Foreign Agricultural Report No. 8, March, 1963. 34 pages.

Relates agricultural diversification to Thai economic development. Shows that Thailand, traditionally a rice monoculture, increased production of crops other than rice (principally corn, cassava, and kenaf) at an average rate of 18 percent per year over the decade 1953-1963.

Buranasiri, Prayad, and Snoh Unakul. "Planning in Thailand: Importance of Political Determination." *The Philippine Economic Journal*, IV, 2, 1965, pp. 335-340.

An interesting commentary on Thai central planning activities by the Secretary-General and the Chief of the Evaluation Division of the Thai central planning agency. The fundamental Thai planning problem, they feel, is the lack of a sense of urgency on the part of Thai leadership.

Cost-Benefit Study of Roads in North and Northeast Thailand. Bangkok: U.S. Agency for International Development, 1966. 39 pages + annexes.

Attempts to determine the comparative cost and economic effect of three road-building projects in North and Northeast Thailand. Analysis is based upon road usage, upon changes in agricultural production and marketing, and upon the growth of village enterprises, land value, and road-construction training. Includes a brief discussion of the effects of roads upon security and village contact with government officials.

Hanks, Lucien M. "The Corporation and the Entourage: A Comparison of Thai and American Social Organization." *Catalyst*, Summer, 1966, pp. 55-63.

Examines the organization and functions of the Thai entourage (or clique) as the Thai counterpart of the Western sociological concept of "corporation." Contrasts authority, recruitment, behavioral and leadership patterns of these two basic social units and discusses the implications of this contrast for the study and planning of economic development in Thailand.

Haring, Joseph E., and Larry E. Westphal. "Financial Policy in Postwar Thailand: External Equilibrium and Domestic Development." *Asian Survey*, May, 1968, pp. 364-377.

Describes the role of Thai financial policy in sustaining growth without inflation in the post-war period. Sketches the steps taken to restore the currency, develop the banking system, promote trade, and stabilize prices without relying on continued trade and exchange controls. Data on prices, income, exchange rates, cost of living, money supply — from pre-World War II to about 1965.

Higher Education and Development in Southeast Asia. See Section F-1.

Hirschman, Albert O. *Development Projects Observed.* Washington, D.C: The Brookings Institute, 1967. 197 pages.

A study of eleven World Bank-financed development projects, one of them an irrigation project in central Thailand, by a distinguished economist in the development field. These are not case studies in the usual sense. Hirschman's purpose was to learn something about project behavior — i.e., the ways in which decision-making is molded and changed by the specific nature of the development project undertaken.

King, John A. *Economic Development Projects and Their Appraisal: Cases and Principles from the Experience of the World Bank.* Baltimore: The Johns Hopkins Press, 1967. 530 pages.

Outlines the Bank's approach to the problems and techniques of project evaluation — viz., economic, technical, managerial, organizational, commercial, and financial. Parts II, III, and IV are devoted to an evaluation of thirty major development projects of the Bank, including the Yanhee multipurpose dam project in Thailand (pp. 191-203), a case illustrating problems of market analysis. A valuable case book.

Loftus, John A. *Reports of the Economic Advisor to the Government of Thailand.* See Section E-1.

Madge, Charles. *Survey Before Development in Thai Villages.* See Section C-5.

Meagher, Robert F. *Public International Development Financing in Thailand.* New York: Columbia University Law School, International Legal Research Program, February, 1963. 103 pages.

An informative study of external development assistance (excluding military aid and suppliers' credits), from 1946 through mid-1962. Describes Thai economic planning and development arrangements up to the early 1960's, and presents a number of case studies of foreign aid in transportation, electric power, and livestock trade. Includes tabular data on U.S. aid to Thailand, 1946-1962; foreign aid to Thailand, 1946-1962; and data on Thailand's six-year plan.

Mitani, Katsumi. "Key Factors in the Development of Thailand," in *Economic Development Issues: Greece, Israel, Taiwan, Thailand.* New York: Committee for Economic Development, 1968, pp. 159-215.

A general survey of economic conditions in Thailand, emphasizing factors contributing to economic stability, and also the roles of education, the Thai-Chinese community, and foreign private investment in regard to economic growth.

Moerman, Michael. "Kinship and Commerce in a Thai-Lao Village." See Section G-1.

Morgan, Theodore, and Nyle Spoelstra (eds.). *Economic Interdependence in Southeast Asia.* Madison: University of Wisconsin Press, 1969. 424 pages.

Papers presented at a conference in Bangkok in 1967. Parts I and V focus on the problems and prospects of economic cooperation in Southeast Asia. (Southeast Asia is broadly defined here to include India, Pakistan, and Ceylon, as well as Hong Kong and Taiwan.) One of the conference papers deals specifically with Thailand: Suparb Yassundara and Yune Huntrakoon, "Some Salient Aspects of Thailand's Trade 1955-64," pp. 127-150.

Muscat, Robert J. *Development Strategy in Thailand: A Study of Economic Growth.* New York: Frederick A. Praeger, 1966. 310 pages.

A broad and informative analysis that seeks to define a

strategy to maximize growth-producing decisions. Considers significant Thai economic features, problems, and opportunities in terms of market characteristics and relationships to an ideal type of market which would presumably nurture economic growth.

Muscat, Robert J. "Growth and the Free Market." *Malayan Economic Review,* April, 1966, pp. 114-125.

Using Thailand as a case in point, examines and refutes the view that economic development and the free market are not compatible.

Myint, Hla. "The Inward and Outward Looking Countries of Southeast Asia and the Economic Future of the Region." See Section E-1.

Northeast Development Plan 1962-1966. Bangkok: National Economic Development Board, n.d. 109 pages + 25 pages of statistical tables.

The basic plan for development of the fifteen Northeastern provinces, approved by the Cabinet in October, 1961. Contains extensive information on many features of the Northeast, authorizes a series of projects, and sets targets for private sector development.

Parker, Glen L. *Accelerating the Rate of Economic Growth: A Study in Economic Policy.* Bangkok: National Economic Development Board, 1963. 299 pages.

Part I of the final report of an industrial advisor to the government of Thailand. Essentially an analysis of institutional problems which impede economic development.

Parker, Glen L. *The Industrial Development of Thailand: A Summary of Recommendations.* Bangkok: National Economic Development Board, 1963. 346 pages.

Part II of the final report of the industrial advisor. Evaluates progress made in industrial development in the early 1960's, and discusses problems of industrial development, along with the advisor's recommendations concerning those problems. This report, like its companion, is primarily concerned with policy, rather than with the analysis of noninstitutional economic characteristics.

Performance Evaluation of Development in Thailand for 1965 under the National Economic Development Plan, 1961-1966. Bangkok: National Economic Development Board, June, 1966. 58 pages.

Data on *Plan* outlays and development expenditures for the year 1965, plus summary statements concerning population and manpower, agriculture and cooperatives, industrial, mineral, and power development, transportation and communications, social welfare, public health and education.

Platenius, Hans. *The Northeast of Thailand: Its Problems and Potentialities.* See Section E-1.

A Public Development Program for Thailand. Baltimore: International Bank for Reconstruction and Development, The Johns Hopkins Press, 1959. 301 pages.

A broad survey of the Thai economy and its social and governmental foundations, prepared by a team of World Bank economists. Includes a "program" or set of recommendations for economic development, laying heavy stress upon the future place of agriculture and the strengthening by government of the economy's infrastructure.

Rozental, Alek A. *Finance and Development in Thailand.* See Section E-1.

Sharp, Lauriston. "Cultural Differences and Southeast Asian Research." See Section G-1.

Siffin, William J. "Economic Development," in Joseph L. Sutton (ed.), *Problems of Politics and Administration in Thailand.* Bloomington: Institute of Training for Public Service, Indiana University, 1962, pp. 125-151.

A nontechnical survey of problems and prospects of economic development in Thailand. Indicates that while a concern with economic development is inevitable, Thailand has not been faced by developmental problems of crisis proportions.

Silcock, T. H. "Outline of Economic Development, 1945-1965," in T. H. Silcock (ed.), *Thailand: Social and Economic Studies in Development.* Canberra: Australian National University Press, 1967, pp. 1-26.

A perceptive summary of Thai economic development over the twenty-year period 1945-1965.

Silcock, T.H. "Promotion of Industry and the Planning Process," in T. H. Silcock (ed.), *Thailand: Social and Economic Studies in Development.* Canberra: Australian National University Press, 1967, pp. 258-288.

Describes efforts to promote industrialization and national planning, focusing on the emergence of state industries, efforts to foster private and foreign investment, and the development of a national planning capacity.

Sitton, Gordon R. *The Role of the Farmer in the Economic Development of Thailand*. Bangkok: First Conference on Agricultural Economics of the Agricultural Economics Society of Thailand, February, 1962, 22 pages. Also issued, New York: Council on Economic Affairs, September, 1962.

Argues that a microeconomic approach, focusing on actions of individual farms and firms, is more fruitful for economic development than the macro-approach, which treats agriculture as a unit. Succinct analysis of needs and opportunities for the continuing development of Thai agriculture through the provision of governmental support and services for farm operators.

The Six Year Economic Development Plan. Bangkok: International Translations, October 28, 1960, pp. 481-487.

This English-language summary of the 1961-1966 national development plan is published as part of the "unofficial" translation of the *Royal Thai Government Gazette*.

Soonthornsima, Chinawoot. "A Macroeconomic Model for Economic Development of Thailand." Unpublished Ph.D. dissertation, University of Michigan, 1963. 189 pages.

Includes a general description of the Thai economy and sets forth a macroeconomic mathematical model which might be used in planning the economic development of Thailand.

Summary of the Second National Economic and Social Development Plan (1967-1971). Bangkok: National Economic Development Board, n.d. 15 pages.

A reproduction of the text of Chapter 1 of the Plan, setting out its forty-five major premises. Calls for emphasis upon private-sector development and increased expenditures in agriculture, particularly for irrigation, and stresses transport and communications development as the largest component in the plan. The plan target calls for an average annual growth in gross (real) domestic product of 8.5 percent per year.

Wharton, Clifton R., Jr. *Research on Agricultural Development in Southeast Asia*. New York: Agricultural Development Council, 1965. 62 pages.

An expanded version of a paper published in the *Journal of Farm Economics*, December, 1963. Includes an inventory of about fifty then-current or recent agricultural economic research studies concerning Thailand.

Wilcox, Clair. *The Planning and Execution of Economic Development in Southeast Asia.* Cambridge: Harvard University Center for International Affairs, 1965. 37 pages.

Includes a three-page discussion of organization for planning in Thailand, with some personal comments on problems of carrying out an effective developmental strategy.

4. Statistical Sources

Advance Report: Household Expenditures Survey B.E. 2505. Bangkok: National Statistical Office, 1963. 105 pages.

A comprehensive report of a two-year survey in the Bangkok-Thonburi metropolitan area based on a sample of 2,500 families. Includes data on family composition, income expenditure, saving, and consumption pattern. Average monthly income of single-person units was 540 baht ($27); for families of eight or more persons the amount was 2,265 baht ($114). For the entire population surveyed, the reported per capita monthly income was 276 baht ($14).

Agricultural Statistics of Thailand. Bangkok: Division of Agricultural Economics, Ministry of Agriculture. First published, 1955; latest known edition, 1961.

Statistical summaries and indices on agricultural production, including rice, timber, forest products, fish, oil seeds, fiber crops, livestock, etc. Agricultural exports information. Data on rainfall, irrigation, population, and income. Considerable variation in reliability of data. Supposed to be published annually. (In Thai and English.)

Amphoe-Tambon Statistical Directory of 14 ARD Changwads. See Section C-5.

Andrews, James M. *Siam: Second Rural Economic Survey, 1934-1935.* See Section E-1.

Annual Economic Report of the Bank of Thailand. Bangkok: Department of Economic Research, Bank of Thailand. Published annually since 1943.

Contains statistics on money and banking, balance of payments, the national budget, and the operations of the Bank of Thailand. Probably the most reliable economic data source in Thailand. (In Thai and English.)

Bulletin of Statistics. Bangkok: National Statistical Office. Published quarterly since 1952.

Statistics on weather, population, education, agriculture, business, trade, transport, money and banking, public revenues and expenditures, and price levels. The different series vary in reliability. (In Thai and English.)

Census of Agriculture. Bangkok: National Statistics Office, 1963.

A series of seventy-two pamphlets, one for each province plus a national summary. Data on area holdings, land tenure, land use, planted and harvested area under cultivation, use of power and agricultural implements, fertilizer, number of livestock and so on.

Changwad-Amphoe Statistical Directory. Bangkok: National Statistical Office, 1965. 75 pages.

Maps and data (crops, occupations, schools, teachers, natural resources, agricultural holdings, population, irrigated crop lands, etc.) on each of seventy-one provinces and their districts. (In Thai and English.)

Economic Survey of Asia and the Far East. Bangkok: Economic Commission for Asia and the Far East. Published annually since 1947.

Since 1957 each issue has examined some major economic problem of the ECAFE region. In addition, current economic conditions are reviewed in each volume of the *Survey*. A valuable reference volume, with its usefulness somewhat limited by the quality of certain data. Most data are from official agencies of the member states.

Education Statistics. See Section F-2.

Land Utilization in Thailand, 1961. Bangkok: Division of Agricultural Economics, Ministry of Agriculture, 1963. 25 pages.

Statistics on land use in Thailand, including data on total land, forest land, swamp and other nontillable land, and farm holdings, by province and region.

Monthly Report. Bangkok: Department of Economic Research, Bank of Thailand.

Current financial statistics, economic notes, and commercial laws and regulations. Includes statistical data on commercial and savings banks, money supply, public debt, bank clearings, wholesale prices, cost of living, exchange rates, and exports and imports. Successor, in January, 1961, to the Bank's *Current Statistics.*

National Income of Thailand, 1965 Edition. Bangkok: National Economic Development Board, June, 1966. 163 pages.

A comprehensive report, including statistical data on the overall economy, consumption expenditure, and capital formation. Statistical series cover the period 1957-1965. Data sources are identified, and computational premises and methods are clearly explained. Revised GNP data indicate a growth rate for the Thai economy, 1957-1963, of 6.9 per cent in constant prices. The first sixty-nine pages of the report are in Thai; explanatory statements and statistical tables are in English.

The Siam Directory. See Section I-3.

Statistical Bibliography: An Annotated Bibliography of Thai Government Statistical Publications. See Section H.

Statistical Yearbook, 1965. Bangkok: National Statistical Office, 1966. 548 pages.

Since 1916, at least, a statistical "yearbook" has been issued by one agency or another of the Thai government. This is the twenty-sixth volume in the series, containing data for recent years up to 1965. Earlier volumes were issued annually or biennially. The 1965 volume, like its predecessors, is a collection of statistics on population, economic activity, and public finance. The statistics must be used with caution.

Thailand: Facts and Figures, 1965. Bangkok: Department of Technical and Economic Cooperation, Ministry of National Development, 1965. 138 pages.

A useful reference volume. Includes a summary of governmental organization and economic characteristics, and sixty-five tables, on money and banking, public finance, trade and exchange, national income, prices, education, and foreign aid.

Thailand: Its Economic Products. Bangkok: Department of Commercial Intelligence, Ministry of Economic Affairs, 1960. 61 pages.

Statistical information about Thai raw materials and industrial products available for purchase by foreign traders.

Thailand Official Yearbook, 1968. See Section A.

Thailand Population Census. Bangkok: National Statistical Office, 1961-1962.

A series of seventy-two pamphlets, one for each province plus a national summary. Each pamphlet contains data on the age, sex, occupation and work status, literacy, education, religion, citizenship, marital status, housing, and place of birth of members of the population. Data are current as of April, 1960. The range of data acquired in the census was limited, but the quality of the statistics seems high. The previous census, taken in 1947, is not of comparable reliability.

Zimmerman, Carl C. *Siam: Rural Economic Survey, 1930-1931.* See Section E-1.

F.
EDUCATION

If education is the *sine qua non* of modernization and social change, then the relative paucity of scholarly attention to education in Thailand is difficult to explain. It may reflect the fact that education is among the most complex of all societal institutions. And we have not gotten around to "disentangling the educational system from other systems in society and specifically identifying those organizations significantly involved in the educational process.... It is both education as process and education as structure that must clearly be delimited before one can proceed very far with any analysis of the relationship between education and any other institution."* In any case, social scientists and professional educators interested in Thailand have produced very little that attempts to relate the Thai education system to the political, economic, or social systems, as shown by the limited number of entries in this section.

The formal education system in Thailand, like those in most developing countries, is an exotic import — or, more accurately, an unmindful blend of British, Continental, and American forms. Volume II of *Higher Education and Development in Southeast Asia* makes this point and gives an adequate profile of Thai postsecondary education. By far the most comprehensive statement of the problems and pressures which, in varying degrees, confront all of the universities of the region is T. H. Silcock's *Southeast Asian University, A Comparative Account of Some Development Problems*. The shorter statements by Fischer and Myint are also well-done.

Two reports of the Michigan State University contract team, *Current and Projected Secondary Educational Programs for*

---

*From Joseph Fischer's lucid essay on education in Indonesia (titled "Indonesia") in James S. Coleman (ed.), *Education and Political Development* (Princeton University Press, 1965), p. 92. While none of the articles in this volume apply specifically to Thailand, it is stimulating throughout — especially the introduction by Coleman and the appended bibliographic guide to education and political socialization by Kenneth I. Rothman.

Thailand: A Manpower and Educational Development Planning Project and *Teachers in Thailand's Universities: An Analysis and Forecast* are worthwhile for the data they contain. The study of the diffusion of innovations in Thai secondary schools by Everett Rogers and others is both interesting and provocative. And the detailed study of the failure of two UNESCO educational projects by Ronald Nairn is especially valuable.

This section is divided into two parts: Part I, higher education, and Part II, elementary and secondary education.

1. Higher Education

Barry, S. J., Jean. *Thai Students in the United States: A Study in Attitude Change.* Ithaca: Cornell University, Southeast Asia Program, Data Paper No. 66, 1967. 160 pages.

A survey of 1,214 Thai students in the United States, which seeks to examine whether student exchange might be beneficial to the socio-economic growth of Thailand. Concludes that students tend to move from a stature and prestige-seeking perspective to a more equalitarian and less conservative view of careers; that they become more family-minded, more self-confident, and more willing to take risks; and also, that they move away from traditional religious concerns toward more nationalistic values, while retaining an underlying stability in religious beliefs or orientation.

Guskin, Alan E., with Tussanee Sookthawee. *Changing Values of Thai College Students.* Bangkok: Faculty of Education, Chulalongkorn University, 1964. 116 pages.

An attitude survey involving a sample of 2,878 male and female students at Chulalongkorn University and nine teacher training colleges. Probes the educational attitudes, occupational expectations, and social value orientations of the group, and provides some suggestive information on attitudes toward security and desires for material achievement. Leaves an impression that the students surveyed aim to work out their futures within the given political system. A study of "values" in a time of change rather than one of changes in values over time.

Guskin, Alan E. "Tradition and Change in a Thai University," in

Education

Robert E. Taylor (ed.), *Cultural Frontiers of the Peace Corps*. Cambridge, Mass.: The M.I.T. Press, 1966, pp. 87-106.

Personal observations and findings from research on attitudes and behavior within a Thai university. Emphasis is placed upon the conflict between traditional Thai culture and Western norms within the university context.

Handbook of Southeast Asian Institutions of Higher Learning. Bangkok: The Association of Southeast Asian Institutions of Higher Learning, 1966. 178 pages.

Describes thirty-five institutions of higher education in Burma, Hong Kong, Indonesia, Malaysia, Philippines, Singapore, Thailand, and Vietnam. Includes descriptions of programs, enrollments, fees, organization, and similar matters for seven Thai institutions.

Higher Education and Development in Southeast Asia. 3 vols. Paris: UNESCO and the International Association of Universities, Vol. I, 1966; Vols. II and III, 1967.

The product of nearly four years of field work, these studies, although uneven in quality and coverage, are the most comprehensive yet done of the role of higher education and its relationship to economic, social and cultural development in the countries of Southeast Asia. Volume I, the *Director's Report*, by Howard Hayden, is essentially a summary of the other three reports. Volume II *Country Profiles*, is a detailed series of educational profiles. Volume III, Part One, by Guy Hunter, discusses high-level manpower for development. Volume III, Part Two, by Richard Noss, is concerned with the problems of language in education.

Maxwell, William E. *Thai Medical Students and Rural Health Service*. See Section G-1.

Myint, Hla. "The Universities of Southeast Asia and Economic Development." *Pacific Affairs*, Summer, 1962. pp. 116-127.

A perceptive appraisal of pressures for expansion and change which confront the universities of Southeast Asia. The consequences for development are examined in terms of (a) the substantial differences between the "need" for university graduates and the effective "demand" for them; (b) the importance of distinguishing between supply and demand factors affecting the post-war student population explosion; and (c) the distinction between education as a socially desirable consumer good and education as an investment in human capital.

Porter, Willis P. *The College of Education, Bangkok, Thailand: A Case Study in Institution Building.* Pittsburgh: Inter-University Program on Institution Building, Graduate School of Public and International Affairs, University of Pittsburgh, 1967. 218 pages.

A case study of the establishment, with American technical and financial assistance, of the first teacher training college in Thailand. Covers the period 1954-1967. The author has been closely associated with the college since its inception.

Schuler, Edgar, and Vibul Thamavit. *Public Opinion Among Thai Students.* Bangkok: Faculty of Social Administration, Thammasat University, 1958. 150 pages + bilingual interview schedule.

An interview study of the opinions and preferences of about four hundred Thai college and university students. Examines the attitudes and aspirations of these students, and suggests little disposition among the group to press for political change. For an analysis of the Schuler-Thamavit findings, see the Mosel article cited in Section G-1.

Shaw, Archibald B., and Thamrong Buasri (eds.). *Teachers in Thailand's Universities: An Analysis and Forecast.* Bangkok: Educational Planning Office, Ministry of Education. East Lansing: Institute for International Studies in Education, Michigan State University, 1968. 92 pages in English.

A study of some 1,807 teaching staff in thirty-two faculties in seven of Thailand's eight degree-granting colleges and universities, based on data provided by the institutions. Suggests that the institutional staff is young, relatively under-educated, not highly motivated, and lightly regarded by the political and bureaucratic elites.

Silcock, T. H. *Southeast Asian University, A Comparative Account of Some Development Problems.* Durham: Duke University Press, 1964. 184 pages.

An authoritative account of the problems of structure, attitudes, standards, research, language, and economics of postcolonial Southeast Asian universities by a professor emeritus of the University of Malaya. Touches on Thai higher education only in passing, although many of the regional problems are relevant to Thai education.

2. Elementary and Secondary Education

An Application of Advanced Technology to the Educational System of a Developing Nation. Los Angeles: Department of Engineering, University of California, 1968. 401 pages.

A report of the 1968 UCLA Engineering Executive Program class presenting a systems-engineering approach for the application of advanced technology (essentially the transmission of information through audio and visual data links) to Thai public education. As a study of the possible uses of advanced audio and visual technologies in mass education, the study is interesting and useful. It says very little, however, about Thai education.

Brembeck, Cole S. *Educational Planning in Thailand.* Paper presented to the Summer Conference on Educational Planning, Syracuse University, July, 1964. 30 pages.

Not examined.

A Cooperative Venture in Teacher Education. Bloomington: Indiana University School of Education, 1963. 111 pages.

The final report of the Indiana University School of Education Agency for International Development assistance project to the College of Education in Bangkok, Thailand. Contractor reports are rarely the most candid or illuminating of documents but this one contains some useful information.

Current and Projected Secondary Education Programs for Thailand: A Manpower and Educational Development Planning Project. Bangkok: Educational Planning Office, Ministry of Education, 1966. 257 pages.

A report on Thai secondary education, with emphasis on its relation to the nation's manpower needs. An outgrowth of a study cited in this section below: *Preliminary Assessment of Education and Human Resources in Thailand.* Prepared with the assistance of a Michigan State University contract team, the report contains recent data on Thai secondary education, along with manpower estimates.

Education Statistics. Bangkok: Division of Educational Techniques, Ministry of Education. Annual.

Statistics on educational finance, salaries, schools, enrollments, teachers, classrooms, students abroad, and related matters. Published in Thai only, 1954-1956; in English and Thai after 1956.

Fischer, Joseph. "Social and Cultural Aspects of Educational Development," SEADAG Papers on Development and Development Policy Problems, No. 9. Southeast Asia Development Advisory Group. New York: The Asia Society, n.d. 11 pages.

An outline of assumptions about and potential approaches to studying the relationship between education and social, cultural, political, and economic change, with specific references made to Thailand. Includes a sharp critique of *Current and Projected Secondary Education Programs for Thailand: A Manpower and Educational Development Planning Project*, cited above.

Fischer, Joseph. "The University Student in South and Southeast Asia." *Minerva*, Autumn, 1963, pp. 39-53.

A perceptive inquiry into the causes and conditions of student unrest, restlessness, and indiscipline in South and Southeast Asia. These, in the main, are said to be: the cleavage between generations, the absence of authoritative models of conduct, the restricted range of opportunities for achievement and conviviality, and the scarcity of socially and economically rewarding opportunities for employment. Not as relevant to Thailand as to Indonesia, Burma and other states in the area, except perhaps as a forecast.

Hatch, Raymond N., and Ampar Jotikasthira. *Vocational Counseling in Secondary Education.* Bangkok: Educational Planning Office, Ministry of Education. East Lansing: Institute for International Studies in Education, Michigan State University, 1966. 76 pages in English.

Prescriptive statement of the need for vocational counseling. Some data on manpower resources and needs.

Nairn, Ronald C. *International Aid to Thailand: The New Colonialism?* New Haven: Yale University Press, 1966. 228 pages.

A valuable case study (which is surprising, given its title) of two UNESCO educational projects — the Cha-Choengsao pilot project and the Thailand UNESCO Fundamental Education Center (TUFEC). Its value lies in a vivid account of the difficulties related to transferring skills from one kind of society to another (e.g., ill-defined project goals, relatively short project life, rapid turnover of personnel, maladaptation to the Thai milieu, and inadequate Thai language skills) and in a demonstration of the importance of host sponsorship to project success: TUFEC was assigned to the Ministry of Education but "this was not where power was located in the Thai hierarchy."

Northeastern Thai and Education. Bangkok: U.S. Agency for International Development, 1968. 7 pages.

A brief summary of published materials and observations concerning educational conditions in the Northeast. Concludes that the generally poor quality of education in the Northeast is the result of many factors, basic among them the lack of teachers, the poor quality of instruction, and the inadequate facilities.

Organization and Management of the Ministry of Education: Survey and Recommendations. See Section D-1.

Preliminary Assessment of Education and Human Resources in Thailand. Bangkok: Joint Thai-U.S. Operations Mission Human Resources Study, U.S. Agency for International Development, 1963. 401 pages.

A survey of Thailand's human resources and an examination of the nation's educational development targets. Part One considers manpower demands and educational supply, and manpower planning and utilization. Part Two contains working papers on manpower and education prepared by the survey team. The report contains data not otherwise available in one place. Essentially a series of fairly rough working papers and planning documents rather than a polished product.

Rogers, Everett, *et al. Diffusion of Innovations: Educational Change in Thai Government Secondary Schools.* East Lansing: Institute for International Studies in Education and Department of Communication, Michigan State University, 1969. 181 pages.

Examines the diffusion of educational innovations from the Thai Ministry of Education, focusing on the distinguishing characteristics of teachers, principals, and provincial education officers who adopt innovations early and perceive them as beneficial. Contains some interesting findings, e.g., the earlier in time schools adopt innovations, the more likely their principals are to be male, be older, have high salaries, have more experience as principals, etc. An interesting and valuable study.

Satorn, Pinyo. "The Provincial School Superintendent in Thailand: A Study of Role Perceptions and Expectations." Unpublished Ph.D. dissertation, Stanford University, 1969.

Investigates the perceptions and expectations held by three groups of Thai administrators of the roles of provincial school superintendents. The three groups were (1) provincial school superintendents; (2) provincial governors; and (3) senior administrators of the Ministry of Education and the Department of Local Administration, Ministry of Interior.

Thambiah, S. J. "Literacy in a Buddhist Village in North-East Thailand." See Section G-1.

Thawisomboon, Sanit, M. L. Pin Malakul, Lam-Toai, and Nguyen Huu Bang. *Education in Thailand and Vietnam.* Honolulu: Institute of Advanced Projects, Translation Series No. 9, East-West Center, University of Hawaii, 1965. 62 pages.

Includes "A Summary of Education in Thailand," outlining the historical development of educational policies and programs and a five-page statement, "Education in Thailand Today." Also contains a brief bibliography.

Wyatt, David K. *The Politics of Reform in Thailand: Education in the Reign of King Chulalongkorn.* See Section B-1.

G.
SOCIO-CULTURAL CHARACTERISTICS OF CONTEMPORARY THAILAND

An appreciation of the basic social and cultural characteristics of a society is essential to understanding almost any of its other aspects. Until recent years an inability to take adequate account of social and cultural diversity has been a major failing of Western scholarship in its application to non-Western areas. It remains a major problem, for although the intimate relationship between man's behavior and his biophysical, social, and cultural environment is today universally acknowledged by scholars, no comprehensive set of perspectives has been developed to account for that relationship, or to guide research or practice. But the situation is improving, as is suggested by the number and the quality of some of the items cited in this section, as well as by items to be found in the journal of the Kyoto University *Center for Southeast Asian Studies,* about which a note will be found in Section I-1.

This section is divided into five parts: (1) Social Structure and Social Change, (2) Religion, (3) Art, Literature, Language, and Drama, (4) Minorities, and (5) Population. In addition, summary statements about Thai society and Thai culture will also be found in the survey materials cited in Section A, in the historical materials cited in Section B, and in materials on subnational government in Section C-5.

1. The Social Structure and Social Change

Advance Report: Household Expenditures Survey B.E. 2505. See Section E-4.

Andrews, James M. *Siam: Second Rural Economic Survey, 1934-1935.* See Section E-1.

Anuman Rajadhon, Phya. *Life and Ritual in Old Siam: Three Studies of Thai Life and Customs.* Translated and edited by William J. Gedney. New Haven: Human Relations Area Files Press, 1961. 191 pages.

　　Includes three essays: "The Life of the Farmer," "Popular Buddhism in Thailand," and "Customs Connected with Birth and the Rearing of Children." Sensitive and sympathetic portraits combine acute reporting with idealized perspective.

Ayal, Eliezer B. "Value Systems and Economic Development in Japan and Thailand." See Section E-3.

Barry, S. J., Jean. *Thai Students in the United States: A Study in Attitude Change.* See Section F-1.

Bell, Peter. "The Role of the Entrepreneur in Economic Development: A Case Study in Thailand." See Section E-3.

Benedict, Ruth F. *Thai Culture and Behavior.* Ithaca: Cornell University, Southeast Asia Program, Data Paper No. 4, 1952. 45 pages.

　　A study done during World War II for the U.S. government, this is a sketch of Thai personality and some basic Thai institutions. Impressionistic and suggestive rather than systematic and definitive.

Blakeslee, D. J., L. W. Huff, and L. W. Kickert. *Village Security Pilot Study.* See Section C-4.

Block, Edward L. "Accelerated Rural Development: A Counter-Insurgency Program in Northeast Thailand." See Section C-4.

Changwad Handbook on Changwad Nakhon Phanom. See Section C-5.

Cruagao, Paitoon. "Changing Thai Society: A Study of the Impact of Urban Cultural Traits and Behavior Upon Rural Thailand." Unpublished Ph.D. dissertation, Cornell University, 1962. 117 pages.

　　Using data from three villages near Lampang, the author examines the hypothesis that rural socio-cultural change is inversely related to social isolation from urban society.

de Young, John E. *Village Life in Modern Thailand.* Berkeley and Los Angeles: University of California Press, 1958. 225 pages.

　　A descriptive account of Thai peasant life in the areas outside the Bangkok delta. Substantial general information on community structure, religion, and economic patterns. A broad survey with many vivid details, rather than an analysis in depth.

Döhring, Karl S. *Siam.* See Section A.

DuBois, Cora. *Social Forces in Southeast Asia.* See Section A.

Embree, John F. "Thailand — A Loosely Structured Social System." *American Anthropologist,* April-June, 1950, pp. 181-193. Reprinted in Evers, *Loosely Structured Social Systems,* cited below.

Perhaps the most cited work on Thailand, this is an impressionistic general sketch of some thematic characteristics of the Thai social system. Considers family characteristics, religion, and patterns of personal relations and captures the flavor of the idea of "permissivity," which seems an important element of Thai social structure. Includes comparisons with Vietnamese and Japanese societies. Embree's "loosely structured" conceptualization has been discounted by scholars such as Mulder, Moerman, and Punyodyana.

Esthetic Perception of Villagers in Northeast Thailand: A Pilot Study. Bangkok: Business Research, Ltd., 1964. 228 pages.

The report of a commissioned survey conducted as part of the data base for planning developmental activities in the Northeast.

Evers, Hans-Dieter. "The Formation of a Social Class Structure: Urbanization, Bureaucratization and Social Mobility in Thailand." *American Sociological Review,* August, 1966, pp. 480-488.

Suggests that urbanization in Thailand may be leading to the formation of a new social class, comprised essentially of a bureaucratic elite. Based upon a 1963 sample survey of high-ranking Thai bureaucrats.

Evers, Hans-Dieter, and T. H. Silcock. "Elites and Selection." See Section C-1.

Evers, Hans-Dieter (ed.). *Loosely Structured Social Systems: Thailand in Comparative Perspective.* New Haven: Yale University, Southeast Asia Studies Cultural Report Series No. 17, 1969. (Distributed by The Cellar Book Shop, 1809 Wyoming, Detroit, Michigan 48221.) 148 pages.

Nine essays and an introduction, focusing upon the applicability of the concept of "loosely structured social system" to

Thailand. Reprints the Embree essay cited herein, and contains original contributions by J. A. Niels Mulder, Herbert P. Phillips, A. Thomas Kirsch, Steven Piker, Boonsanong Punyodyana, Clark E. Cunningham, Hans-Dieter Evers, and Michael Moerman. A bibliography is also included.

Fraser, Thomas M., Jr. *Fishermen of South Thailand: The Malay Villagers.* See Section C-5.

Fraser, Thomas M., Jr. *Rusembilan: A Malay Fishing Village in Southern Thailand.* See Section C-5.

Freyn, Hubert. "Culture and Economics in Thailand." *Far Eastern Economic Review,* January 12, 1961, pp. 48-49, 52-53.

A thoughtful sketch, by a noneconomist, who outlines some cultural characteristics of present-day Thailand, notes some of the looming economic problems, and concludes, "What man requires as a rule to change his ingrained customs and ideas is pressure, internal or external. In Thailand this pressure has so far been absent."

Goldsen, Rose K., and Max Ralis. *Factors Relating to Acceptance of Innovations in Bang Chan, Thailand.* Ithaca: Cornell University, Southeast Asia Program, Data Paper No. 24, 1957. 72 pages.

This systematic small-group study is concerned only implicitly with political change, but the implications are provocative. Carefully examines the association of certain social, cultural, economic, communications, and attitudinal factors with the acceptance of certain specific innovations in a particular village. No firm answers about means of effecting political change, but the study does imply certain hypotheses about impediments to and opportunities for political mobilization.

Graham, Henry and Juanita. *Some Changes in Thai Family Life.* Bangkok: Institute of Public Administration, Thammasat University, 1957. 55 pages.

A study of family life among a stratum of urban Thais by an American social welfare administrator and teacher and his wife, a psychiatric social worker, based upon 107 interviews.

Guskin, Alan E., with Tussanee Sookthawee. *Changing Values of Thai College Students.* See Section F-1.

Hanks, Lucien M. "American Aid Is Damaging Thai Society." *Trans-Action,* October, 1968, pp. 29-34.

An insightful and novel conceptualization of the Thai social order and the destabilizing effects of American military assistance on it. Hanks likens the Thai social order to "a bundle of fine golden chains of varying lengths, with only occasional cross-connections." The structure is "loose" only horizontally, not from top to bottom. With respect to public and semipublic agencies, the length, strength, and durability of any given "chain" depends upon the degree of monopolistic hold it has on some public service or function.

Hanks, Lucien M. "The Corporation and the Entourage: A Comparison of Thai and American Social Organization." See Section E-3.

Hanks, Lucien M., and Herbert P. Phillips, "A Young Thai from the Countryside: A Psychosocial Analysis," in B. Kaplan (ed.), *Studying Personality Crossculturally.* Evanston: Row, Peterson, 1961, pp. 637-656.

A case study plus generalizations about the manner in which status differentiation provides coherence in the Thai social system. Asserts that "group coherence depends upon status inequality...." An equal "stands as a potential competitor for favors. Group solidarity requires...framing unambiguously the relative rank of each."

Hanks, Lucien M., Jr. "Merit and Power in the Thai Social Order." *American Anthropologist,* December, 1962, pp. 1247-1261.

An important contribution to an understanding of contemporary Thai social structure. Outlines dominant features of social structure and explains how both mobility and stability are persisting features of the system.

Hauck, Hazel M. *Aspects of Health, Sanitation and Nutritional Status in a Siamese Rice Village: Studies in Bang Chan, 1952-1954.* Ithaca: Cornell University, Southeast Asia Program, Data Paper No. 22, 1956. 73 pages.

Examines the general condition of health and sanitation of the village of Bang Chan, and the nutritional status of 166 persons in a random sample of 31 village households and 233 primary school children. Concludes that, because modern medicine probably will not be readily available to the majority of villagers for many years, emphasis should be placed upon teaching the people through existing village leaders and practitioners to adopt improved health practices.

Hauck, Hazel M. *Maternal and Child Health in a Siamese Rice*

Village: Nutritional Aspects. Ithaca: Cornell University, Southeast Asia Program, Data Paper No. 39, 1959. 70 pages.

Information on health, care, and diet of mothers and small children in the village of Bang Chan. In all, sixty-six mothers of young children were interviewed.

Hauser, Philip M. "Cultural and Physical Obstacles to Economic Development in the Less Developed Areas." See Section E-1.

Hindley, Donald. "Thailand: The Politics of Passivity." See Section C-1.

Impact of Television Ownership on Other Media Habits of Respondents in Bangkok-Thonburi. Bangkok: U.S. Information Agency, 1964. 58 pages.

A nonprobability sample survey of radio and television ownership in 522 households in the nine most heavily populated districts of Bangkok. An effort was made to assess the possible impact of television on viewers' use of other communications media — e.g., radio, motion pictures, magazines, newspapers, and books. Owing to limitations of method and interview technique, the reliability of some of the data is questionable.

Innovations in Ubol Changwad. Bangkok: U.S. Agency for International Development, 1966. 25 pages + 3 annexes.

Studies the diffusion of information about technical assistance programs and the spread of innovations in this northeastern Changwad. The innovators are identified and described. Annexes contain studies of the Accelerated Rural Development Program, farm debts, and farmers' credit organizations in the provinces.

Jacobs, Milton, Farhad Farzanegan, and Alexander R. Askenasy. "A Study of Key Communicators in Urban Thailand." *Social Forces,* December, 1966, pp. 192-199.

Identifies (in order of decreasing importance) the key communicators in four cities of Thailand as monks, professionals, military men, governmental officials, teachers, and merchants. The most critical characteristics were found to be education, heavy exposure to the mass media, and roles in word-of-mouth communication.

Judd, Lawrence C. *Dry Rice Agriculture in Northern Thailand.* See Section E-1.

Judd, Lawrence C. "A Study of the Cultural Organization of Tong Taa Village in Thailand." See Section C-5.

Karnjanaprakorn, Choop. *Community Development and Local Government in Thailand*. Bangkok: Institute of Public Administration, Thammasat University, 1965. 65 pages.

　Paper prepared for a seminar at the East-West Center, University of Hawaii. Particularly useful for its discussion from a Thai perspective of problems of bureaucratic authority and leadership in relation to social-change objectives.

Kaufman, Howard K. *Bangkhuad: A Community Study in Thailand*. New York: J. J. Augustin, for the Association for Asian Studies, 1960. 235 pages.

　No stable and systematic stratification pattern has been detected in Thai village studies, but many scholars have commented upon the presence of a graded status hierarchy. Kaufman notes a number of status-respect relationships in this study of Bangkhuad. "1. abbot-monk; 2. monk-laymen; 2a. monk-laywomen; 3. village headman-farmer; 4. district officer-villagers; 5. district officer-village headman; 6. commune headman-village headman; 7. teacher-pupil; 8. teacher-villager; 9. head school teacher-teacher; 10. storekeeper-customer; 11. dekwat (temple boy)-lay children; 12. doctor-laity." See also Section C-5.

Keyes, Charles F. "Ethnic Identity and Loyalty of Villagers in Northeast Thailand." *Asian Survey*, July, 1966, pp. 362-369.

　Examines self-perceived ethnic identities and loyalties of northeastern villagers, drawing from field studies in Changwad Mahasarakham, Roi-et, and Kalasin. Notes the rapid waning of localism, and notes that, while many villagers identify themselves as Isan or Lao to differentiate themselves from the Central Thais, they do not automatically base their national identities upon this ethnic premise.

Keyes, Charles F. *Isan: Regionalism in Northeastern Thailand*. Ithaca: Cornell University, Southeast Asia Program, Data Paper No. 65, 1967. 86 pages.

　A valuable, systematic statement of the history and contemporary socio-political characteristics of one of the major regions of Thailand. The author's aim is "to clarify how the people of northeastern Thailand fit within the context of a Thai State."

Keyes, Charles F. "Land Tenure in Thailand: Legal Definitions and Peasant Practice." Paper delivered to a symposium on the Impact of Land Tenure Changes upon Social Structure in Developing Nations, Seattle, June 16, 1969. 23 pages.

A detailed description of land registration arrangements and a perceptive analysis of a looming problem — i.e., poor specification of customary and legal systems of land tenure, as a result of inadequacies in the operation of the legal system.

Keyes, Charles F. *Local Leadership in Rural Thailand.* See Section C-1.

Keyfitz, Nathan. "Political-Economic Aspects of Urbanization in South and Southeast Asia." See Section C-5.

Kingshill, Konrad. *Ku Daeng — The Red Tomb. A Village Study in Northern Thailand.* See Section C-5.

Klausner, William. "*Nak aw, bao su,* The Work Cycle in a Northeastern Thai Village." *Social Science Review* (Bangkok), June, 1966, pp. 48-59.

"*Nak aw, bao su*" means, approximately, "No matter how hard the work, we can do it." Describes in detail the annual work cycle of the village of Nong Khon, in Ubol province, and strikes at a rather common misconception: that northeastern Thais plant a rice crop and after the harvest do little or nothing. In Nong Khon villagers work on as many as three rice crops including upland rice, prepare salt, garden, and generally participate in an almost uninterrupted annual work cycle.

Landon, Kenneth P. *Siam in Transition.* See Section B-1.

le May, Reginald S. *An Asian Arcady: The Land and People of Northern Siam.* Cambridge: W. Heffner, 1926. 274 pages.

Perceptive descriptions of the history and peoples of northern Thailand. Has been described as "*the* standard work on Northern Siam."

le May, Reginald S. *The Culture of South-East Asia.* See Section G-3.

le May, Reginald S. (trans.) *Siamese Tales Old and New: The Four Riddles and Other Stories. With Some Reflections on the Tales.* See Section G-3.

Luykx, Nicolaas G. M. "Some Comparative Aspects of Rural Public Institutions in Thailand, the Philippines, and Viet Nam." See Section C-5.

Maxwell, William E. *Thai Medical Students and Rural Health Service.* Honolulu: Institute of Advanced Projects, East-West Center, University of Hawaii, 1967. 104 pages.

The report of a statistical and attitudinal survey of Thai

medical students, excerpted from a doctoral dissertation study for the Department of Sociology, UCLA.

Moerman, Michael. *Agricultural Change and Peasant Choice in a Thai Village.* See Section E-1.

Moerman, Michael. "Ban Ping's Temple: The Center of a Loosely Structured Society," in Manning Nash, *et al.*, *Anthropological Studies in Theravada Buddhism.* New Haven: Yale University, Southeast Asia Studies, Cultural Report No. 13, 1966, pp. 137-174.

Questions the value of two "standard principles" of Thai society: (a) that village society is loosely structured (Embree), and (b) that the temple is at its center (Landon, Blanchard, and others).

Moerman, Michael. "Kinship and Commerce in a Thai-Lue Village." *Ethnology,* October, 1966, pp. 360-364.

Examines social and economic change in a northern Thai village, and notes that the content but not the form of economic transactions is changing in the process of modernization. Underlines the persistence of traditional socio-economic patterns of commerce despite the introduction of new commodities.

Moerman, Michael. "A Thai Village Headman as a Synaptic Leader." *Journal of Asian Studies,* May, 1969, pp. 535-549.

A study of the role of the headman in Ban Ping, a Thai-Lue village, based on data collected during 1959-1961. Argues that the relationship between the village headman's synaptic leadership and the village's corporateness provides a focus for investigating how rural villages are incorporated into developing nations. Provides the greatest detail on the recruitment to and performance of this synaptic role that exists in the literature.

Moerman, Michael. "Western Culture and the Thai Way of Life," in *Asia: A Selection of Papers Delivered Before the Asia Society.* New York: The Asia Society, 1964, pp. 31-50.

A perceptive and well-informed characterization of the "developmental" impact of the West on Thai rural life, including descriptions of rural economy and rural economic behavior.

Mosel, James N. "Communication Patterns and Political Socialization in Transitional Thailand," in Lucian W. Pye (ed.), *Communications and Political Development.* Princeton: Princeton University Press, 1963, pp. 184-228.

An acute analysis of relationships between communications media and political socialization. Also examines receptivity and predisposition to political change within Thai society.

Mulder, J. A. Niels. *Monks, Merit and Motivation: An Exploratory Study of the Social Functions of Buddhism in Thailand in Processes of Guided Social Change.* DeKalb: Center for Southeast Asian Studies, Northern Illinois University, 1969. 43 pages.

Examines possible relationships between Buddhism and Buddhist institutions and processes of stimulated social and economic change in Thai rural society. Notes the increasing involvement of the Sangha in socio-economic development in rural Thailand, but asserts that the monks, as agents of change, should not be studied as a homogeneous group but rather at two distinct levels, i.e., the national and the village levels.

Noranitipadungkarn. *Elites, Power Structure and Politics in Thai Communities.* See Section C-5.

Phillips, Herbert P. "The Election Ritual in a Thai Village." See Section C-1.

Phillips, Herbert P. *Thai Peasant Personality: The Patterning of Interpersonal Behavior in the Village of Bang Chan.* Berkeley and Los Angeles: University of California Press, 1965. 231 pages.

A portrait based upon data from a particular village. But the substantial, if tentative, generalizations probably are justified. Data were collected through the use of a sentence-completion interview technique. The work of a perceptive and discerning scholar, as well as an important application of social-science methodology to research in Thailand. An extensive discussion of methodology is included.

Piker, Steven. "Character and Socialization in a Thai Peasant Community." Unpublished Ph.D. dissertation, University of Washington, 1964.

Basically a study of child socialization in the village of Banoi, Ayutthaya Province, couched in terms of the "culture and personality" school of anthropology. Draws certain conclusions about interpersonal relations among Banoi villagers, the most significant of which note the (1) pervasive sense of insecurity and distrust, and a concomitant sense of personal isolation; (2) profound aversion to anything resembling open or direct expression of hostility or animosity in interpersonal relations; and (3) ambivalence toward dependency postures as a solution to many problems of adulthood.

Piker, Steven. "The Relationship of Belief Systems to Behavior in Rural Thai Society." See Section G-2.

Piker, Steven. "Sources of Stability and Instability in Rural Thai Society." *Journal of Asian Studies*, August, 1968, pp. 777-790.

Examines "dependence-independence" ambivalence in the Thai peasant social structure (noted also by Hanks and Phillips in earlier studies); identifies the points at which the traditional integration of rural Thai society is breaking down under the pressures of modernization; and suggests the institutional and characterological factors with which any synthesis must come to terms.

Saund, Dalip. "Ban Khua Kaj: A Case Study of the Response to Development in a Northeast Thai Village." Unpublished Ph.D. dissertation, University of California at Los Angeles, 1969. 219 pages.

This study of the impact of recent governmental development programs on a Northeast village argues that they lead villagers to develop a new model of government official-peasant relations which includes "concepts of free and open communication between peasant and official, cooperation, and official service to the peasant population." Because this new model represents a marked departure from past experience, villagers tend to distinguish between "traditional" officials, usually represented by regular local officials and police, and officials who fit the new model, usually represented by agents of the development programs.

Schuler, Edgar, and Vibul Thamavit. *Public Opinion Among Thai Students*. See Section F-1.

Seidenfaden, Major Erik. *The Thai Peoples*. Bangkok: The Siam Society, 1958. 117 pages.

A well-informed ethnographic study which describes the groups and subgroups that comprise the Thai populace. Published posthumously, it is the work of a man who spent some forty years in Thailand, part of that time attached to the Royal Siamese Provincial Gendarmerie.

Sharp, Lauriston. "Cultural Differences and Southeast Asian Research," in *American Research on Southeast Asian Development: Asian and American Views, a Special Report by The*

Asia Society. New York: The Asia Society, 1968, pages 65-79.

Calls for a less Western-oriented research approach to the cultural systems of Southeast Asia: "It is in the cultural areas, sentiments and values that most native and foreign research workers...are most hampered by the impediments of ignorance and misunderstanding." Offers a perceptive commentary on the Thai area handbooks, plus a shrewd analysis of the Thai-Chinese symbiosis for the modernization of Thailand.

Sharp, Lauriston, Hazel Hauck, Kamol Janlekha, and Robert Textor. *Siamese Rice Village: A Preliminary Study of Bang Chan, 1948-1949*. Bangkok: Cornell Research Center, 1953. 300 pages.

An initial report on the findings of the Cornell research project at Bang Chan, giving substantial information on the socio-cultural characteristics of the village, as well as on its relation to official government in Thailand.

Sharp, Lauriston. "Peasants and Politics in Thailand." See Section C-1.

Silcock, T. H. *Proud and Serene*. Canberra: Australian National University Press, 1968. 123 pages.

A collection of character sketches of individual Thais — farmers, village school teachers, government officials, children, a poetess, and the Governor of the Bank of Thailand — by a keen observer of the Thai scene.

"Symposium on Northeast Thailand." See Section G-4.

Tambiah, S. J. "Literacy in a Buddhist Village in North-East Thailand," in Jack Goody (ed.), *Literacy in Traditional Societies*. Cambridge: Cambridge University Press, 1968, pp. 85-131.

A very detailed analysis of traditional and contemporary literacy in a village in Udon province.

Textor, Robert B. *From Peasant to Pedicab Driver*. New Haven: Yale University, Southeast Asia Studies, 1961. 83 pages.

A study of a significant migrant group which moved in sizeable numbers from Northeast Thailand to Bangkok to work as pedicab (samlor) operators, often returning to their homes after an interval of working.

Thai Local Administration: A Study of Villager Interaction with Community and Amphoe Administration. See Section C-5.

Van Roy, Edward. *On the Theory of Corruption.* Unpublished manuscript, Department of Economics, SUNY, Stony Brook, N.Y. 32 pages. (Forthcoming in *Economic Development and Cultural Change.*)

Consists of three sections. The first outlines alternative conceptual approaches to the study of corruption — viz., ethnocentric, functionalist, and evolutionist — in terms of their degrees of relevance to the question: Why is corruption a universal phenomenon despite its universal abhorence? The second and third sections apply these approaches to the specific case of Thailand. The importance of "connections" in Thai economic and social organization is used to identify the indigenous locus of corruption. An interesting and useful addition to a sparse and emotion-laden literature.

Vella, Walter F. *The Impact of the West on Government in Thailand.* See Section B-2.

Wijeyewardene, Gehan. "A Note on Irrigation and Agriculture in a North Thai Village," Vol. II in *Felicitation Volumes of Southeast Asian Studies.* Bangkok: The Siam Society, 1965, pp. 255-259.

A short note on the social unit (extended families) which manages agricultural production in a northern Thai village.

Wijeyewardene, Gehan. "Some Aspects of Rural Life in Thailand," in T. H. Silcock (ed.), *Thailand: Social and Economic Studies in Development.* Canberra: Australian National University Press, 1967, pp. 65-83.

An excellent general description of kinship, marriage, divorce, village structure and organization, attitudes toward land, religion, and politics in rural Thailand. Concludes, in agreement with other analysts, that neither kinship nor locality is the basis of organization in rural Thai society. The tables on land holdings are particularly worthwhile.

Yatsushiro, Toshio. *Studies of Northeast Villages in Thailand.* See Section C-5.

Yatsushiro, Toshio. *Village Organization and Leadership in Northeast Thailand.* See Section C-5.

104　　Thailand: Politics, Economy, and Socio-Cultural Setting

2. Religion

Alabaster, Henry. *The Wheel of the Law*. London: Trubner, 1871. 323 pages.

    An old source, interesting and informative on aspects of "practical Buddhism" in Thailand a century ago.

Attagara, Kingkeo. *The Folk Religions of Ban Nai, A Hamlet in Central Thailand*. Bangkok: Kurusapha Press, 1968. (Originally Ph.D. dissertation, Indiana University, 1967).

    A study of the oral tradition of the people of Ban Nai hamlet in Cholburi province, Central Thailand. Includes a description of the village and commentary on beliefs, rites, and themes in the oral tradition. The bulk of the study follows, consisting of about four hundred printed pages of folklore texts, essentially unedited, obtained from twenty-one informants. These are grouped into several categories: ordinary folktales, epics, legends, historical tales, and ceremonial songs. There is a total of 128 items, of which about eighty are common folklore.

Bradley, William L. *An Introduction to Comparative Religion*. Bangkok: Thammasat University Press, 1965. 275 pages.

    This book, written for the use of students in the first year Liberal Arts Faculty at Thammasat University, draws many of its illustrations from Theravada Buddhism. The comparisons are made between religious approaches, or world views, rather than between whole religions. The author was a visiting scholar at Thammasat University during the writing.

Burtt, Edwin A. (ed.). *The Teachings of the Compassionate Buddha*. New York: New American Library of World Literature, Mentor Books, 1955. 247 pages.

    Includes about forty-five pages of selections illustrative of "The Spirit of Theravada Buddhism." As in the case of the Bradley book, cited above, this is a useful source which concerns doctrines and perspectives rather than religious institutions.

Cady, John F. *Thailand, Burma, Laos, and Cambodia*. See Section A.

Evers, Hans-Dieter. *Organizational Structure and Social Environment: A Comparative Study of Buddhist Monastic Organization of Ceylon and Thailand*. DeKalb: Center for Southeast

Asian Studies, Northern Illinois University, 1967. 40 pages.

A theoretical statement; its orientation is indicated by a key proposition: "The more formalized and strict the structure of a society, the less formalized and strict is the structure of formal organizations whose organizational goals are compatible with the norms and values of that society." Evers infers that "The role of the Buddhist Sangkha as a formal organization...is...precarious." A shorter version of this essay appeared in *Sociologus*, Vol. 18, No. 1, 1968, pp. 20-35.

Finegan, Jack. *The Background of Buddhism, Confucianism, Taoism.* Vol. II, in *The Archeology of World Religions.* Princeton: Princeton University Press, 1965 (1952). 599 pages + 110 plates.

Encyclopedic surveys of the origin and growth of Buddhism, Confucianism, and Taoism in their historical contexts, with an emphasis on archaeological materials and basic literary documents. Relevant as a general orientation.

Ingersoll, Jasper C. "The Priest and the Path: An Analysis of the Priest Role in a Central Thai Village." Unpublished Ph.D. dissertation, Cornell University, 1963.

Using a "role theory" perspective, characterizes the duties, style of behavior, norms, and values of the priest, and examines the influences of learning, recruitment, change, and stability on his role. Based on extensive field study in a community near Nakorn Phanom on the central basin, this is a valuable source of insight and information concerning the pervasive place of religion in the Thai culture and the manifest pattern of institutionalized Thai Buddhism.

Ishii, Yoneo. "Church and State in Thailand." *Asian Survey*, October, 1968, pp. 864-871.

Traces briefly the relationship between church and state in Thailand from the early days of the absolute monarchy to Sarit. Concludes that the church today is subordinate to and largely dependent upon the material and moral support of the state.

Jayanama, Direck. "Buddhism and Administration." Bangkok: Mahamakuta Rajavidyalaya Printing Press, 1956, 22 pp. Originally presented as paper at the U.S. Information Center, Bangkok, May 21, 1956; also reprinted in Bangkok *Standard*, No. 491, May 26, 1956, pp. 18 ff., and June, 1956, pp. 22-23.

A perceptive, impressionistic commentary on some of the ways in which Buddhism appears to affect administration in Thailand.

Kirsch, A. Thomas. "Phu Thai Religious Syncretism: A Case Study of Thai Religion and Society." Unpublished Ph.D. dissertation, Harvard University, 1967.

A superb, detailed study of the religion of a Phu Thai village concerned with showing how the three religious subsystems of "animism," "folk brahmanism," and Buddhism are integrated into a syncretic system dominated by Buddhist concepts. While the study concerns one village, Kirsch finds implications for the whole of Thai society.

Klausner, William. "Popular Buddhism in Northeast Thailand," in F. S. C. Northrop and H. H. Livingston (eds.), *Cross Cultural Understandings: Epistemology in Anthropology.* New York: Harper & Row, 1964.

A summary of Buddhism as it exists in northeastern Thai villages by an experienced observer of northeastern Thai peasant society. Nearer to the ideal system as conceived by northeastern peasants than it is to a sociological analysis of religious behavior.

Landon, Kenneth P. "Modern Trends in Siamese Culture." Unpublished Ph.D. dissertation, University of Chicago, 1938. 264 pages.

A historical survey, tracing the evolution of Thai Buddhism and its involvement with spirit cults and Brahmanism, outlining the religious reforms of King Mongkut, and generally offering a useful introduction to the subject of Thai Buddhism.

Landon, Kenneth P. *Southeast Asia, Crossroad of Religion.* Chicago: University of Chicago Press, 1949. 215 pages.

Chapter Four, "Siam, a Hinduized Nation," sketches ancient Thai history and the impact of Hindu civilization on Thailand.

Lavangkura, Yen. "The Administration of Religious Affairs: A Study of the Relationship Between the Government and the Sangha in Thailand." Unpublished Master's thesis. Bangkok: Institute of Public Administration, Thammasat University, 1962. 181 pages.

Describes formal relations between the Sangha, a partially self-governing religious organization, and the Thai government.

le May, Reginald S. *A Concise History of Buddhist Art in Siam.* See Section G-3.

Life of the Buddha According to Thai Temple Paintings. Bangkok: U.S. Information Service, 1957. 184 pages.

The unique volume produced under the direction of Dr. Kurt F. Leidecker with the cooperation of a number of the members of the Thai Buddhist order. Sixty-five temple paintings are reproduced in color, having been copied and in many cases extensively restored by Rudolph W. E. Hampe. Descriptions of the paintings — actually, of episodes in the saga of the Buddha — were prepared by members of the Thai Sangha, who also provide rich insights into the substance of the Buddhist legend, which is a vital element of Thai tradition. The volume records an art form which is fading away as the elements destroy many of the old paintings. (In Thai and English.)

Mulder, J. A. Niels. *Monks, Merit and Motivation: An Exploratory Study of the Social Functions of Buddhism in Thailand in Processes of Guided Social Change.* See Section G-1.

The Patimokkha: 227 Fundamental Rules of a Bhikkhu. Bangkok: Social Science Association Press, 1966. 119 pages.

An introduction by Phra Sasana Sobhana, head bhikkhu of Wat Borovanives Vihara, explains the tradition behind the rules; selected Tipitaka texts, providing further explanation of the rules, are included. The rules are set forth in English and a version of Anglicized Thai. Appendices include a collection of suttas and gathas usually chanted after recitation of the patimokkha, an abbreviated form of patimokkha recitation, and a set of commentaries on various aspects of the patimokkha. Pali translation of the rules and chants is by Ven. Nanamoli Thera.

Pfanner, David E., and Jasper Ingersoll. "Theravada Buddhism and Village Economic Behavior, A Burmese and Thai Comparison." *Journal of Asian Studies,* May, 1962, pp. 341-361.

A report based on field studies in a Burmese and a Thai village in 1959-1960. Using an anthropological perspective, examines the interrelations of religious roles and economic activities.

Piker, Steven. "The Relationship of Belief Systems to Behavior in Rural Thai Society." *Asian Survey,* May, 1968, pp. 384-399.

Argues that the observed correspondences between the content of Thai magico-animistic beliefs and the orientation of Thai peasants to the mundane world lies not so much in the prepotency of religious ideas as in the ontogeny of Thai peasant personality.

Prinyayogavipulya, Luang. *Concise Principles of Buddhism.*

Bangkok: Foundation for Education in the Art of Right Living (Sammajivasilpa Mulnidhi, 744 Phya Nag Lane, Phya Tai Road), 1957. 29 pages.

This little booklet, published with the assistance of the Asia Foundation, was prepared by an acknowledged Buddhist scholar. A useful small catechism of Thai Buddhist tenets.

Schecter, Jerrold. *The New Face of Buddha.* New York: Coward-McCann, 1967. 300 pages.

A readable and interesting account of the force and place of contemporary Buddhism in Southeast Asia by the chief of the *Time-Life* Tokyo bureau. Concludes that the political strength of Buddhism lies in its activism within the individual Buddhist countries and not on the international political level. One chapter specifically devoted to Thai Buddhism.

Von der Mehden, Fred. *Religion and Nationalism in Southeast Asia.* See Section A.

Wells, Kenneth E. *History of Protestant Work in Thailand.* Bangkok: Church of Christ in Thailand (14 Pramuan Road, Bangkok). 213 pages.

A relatively brief but well-written history, by a man who first came to Thailand as a missionary in 1927.

Wells, Kenneth E. *Thai Buddhism, Its Rites and Activities.* Bangkok: Bangkok Times Press, 1939. 284 pages. Bangkok: Bangkok Christian Bookstore, 1960. 320 pages.

A valuable study of Thai Buddhism, relevant to any effort to understand "practical Buddhism" with its ceremonies, rites, and institutional qualities.

Yatsushiro, Toshio. *Drought in the Northeast and the Rain-Making Ceremony.* Bangkok: U.S. Agency for International Development, August, 1966. 6 pages.

A brief, perceptive description of a ceremony undertaken in response to a critical water shortage.

3. Art, Language, Literature, and Drama

Bowie, Theodore (ed.). *The Arts of Thailand.* Bloomington: Indiana University and others, 1960. 219 pages.

Subtitled: *A Handbook of the Architecture, Sculpture and*

Painting of Thailand (Siam) and a Catalog of the Exhibition in the United States in 1960-61-62. Includes an essay with illustrations, "The Architecture and Sculpture of Siam," by A. B. Griswold, pp. 27-181. Notes for the catalog of the exhibition, pp. 183-213, were written by M. C. Subhadradis Diskul.

Brown, James Marvin. *From Ancient Thai to Modern Dialects.* Bangkok: Social Science Association Press of Thailand, 1965. ix, 180 pages + charts.

A theoretical linguistic analysis of the evolution of the phonological system of modern Thai and modern Thai dialects. Impressively systematic and apparently sophisticated in method.

Campbell, Stuart. *The Fundamentals of the Thai Language.* New York: Paragon Book Gallery, 1964. 523 pages.

An introduction to the Thai language for English-speaking foreigners. Provides a useful English-Thai vocabulary and information on the construction of simple sentences. The Thai alphabet and tonal system are treated extensively.

Gedney, William J. "Thailand and Laos," in Thomas A. Sebeok, *et al.* (eds.), *Linguistics in East Asia and South East Asia,* Vol. II of *Current Trends in Linguistics.* Paris and The Hague: Mouton, 1967, pp. 782-814.

An informative survey essay that notes and comments on descriptive, historical, comparative, and dialectic studies of Thai. Includes a nonannotated bibliography of more than one hundred selected items.

Griswold, Alexander B. *Dated Buddha Images of Northern Siam.* Ascona, Switzerland: Artibus Asiae, 1959. 66 pages, 12 figures, and 57 plates.

Through extensive study of a group of Buddhist images found in Northern Thailand, the author sets forth the hypothesis that the pre-Sukothai "school" of art was actually a late fifteenth-century part of the Sukothai period rather than a thirteenth-century school of art in its own right. Describes the socio-economic setting of this "Golden Age" of Thai art, as well as the Buddha images themselves.

Haas, Mary R. *The Thai Reader.* Washington, D.C.: American Council of Learned Societies, Program in Oriental Languages, Publication Series A — Texts — No. 1, 1954. 223 pages.

Designed to cover the intermediate level of instruction in Thai. Lessons 1-46 consist of short readings on Thailand's society and culture. Lessons 47-50 introduce the student to Thai newspaper reading.

Haas, Mary R. *The Thai System of Writing*. Washington, D.C.: American Council of Learned Societies, Program in Oriental Languages, Publication Series D — Aids — No. 5, 1956. 115 pages.

A completely revised version of the author's 1952 volume of the same title. The written Thai is accompanied by phonetic transcription to facilitate the association of the written work with its pronunciation. Designed to be used in conjunction with *The Thai Reader* and *Thai Vocabulary*, also written by the author.

Haas, Mary R. *Thai Vocabulary*. Washington, D.C: American Council of Learned Societies, Program in Oriental Languages, Publication Series A — Texts — No. 2, 1955. 189 pages.

A short English-Thai dictionary for beginning and intermediate-level students of Thai. Contains vocabulary items from *The Thai Reader* and selected words from other sources.

Haas, Mary R., and Heng R. Subhanka. *Spoken Thai*. New York: Henry Holt, 1954. 701 pages.

A compilation of commonly used Thai words and phrases for the student of Thai or the foreign traveler in Thailand. Designed to be used in conjunction with a series of phonograph records.

Klausner, William J. "Ceremonies and Festivals in a Northeastern Thai Village." *Social Science Review* (Bangkok), September, 1966, pp. 1-12.

A description of ceremonies and festivals in Ban Nong, Amphur Muang, Ubol, by an experienced observer of the Thai cultural milieu.

le May, Reginald. *A Concise History of Buddhist Art in Siam*. Rutland, Vermont: Charles E. Tuttle Company, 1962. 169 pages + 205 plates.

An extensive, chronologically ordered survey of Thai Buddhist art to the Ayudhya Period. The author describes not only the art, but its political and social settings. Includes a critique of A. B. Griswold's hypothesis concerning the pre-Sukothai School (see A. B. Griswold. *Dated Buddha Images of Northern Siam*, this section.). Contains an extensive bibliography of works on Buddhist art and its history.

le May, Reginald S. *The Culture of South-East Asia*. London:

George Allen and Unwin, 1954. 222 pages, many illustrations.

This comprehensive survey traces the evolution of temples and art forms from Indian sources into Malaya, Sumatra, Java, Cambodia, and Thailand. It also provides data about the broader cultural and social context, and is the definitive work in its area.

le May, Reginald S. (trans.). *Siamese Tales Old and New: The Four Riddles and Other Stories. With Some Reflections on the Tales.* London: Doublas, 1930; A. Probsthain, 1958, 192 pages. Paperback edition: *Thai Tales Old and New,* "Printed in Shanghai, 1945," 153 pages.

A delightful retelling of fifteen traditional tales, offering insight into the perspective of Thais of the Central Basin and the North. Author's comments on Thai culture occupy about a third of the volume.

Life of the Buddha According to Thai Temple Paintings. See Section G-2.

Mosel, James N. *A Survey of Classical Thai Poetry: Commentary on Thai Text to Accompany a Tape-Recording of Thai Poetry.* Bangkok, 1959. 24 pages.

Describes the content and form of the poetry, often relating them to social characteristics of the period. Presents examples of the poetry in Thai. (Upon request, the accompanying tape recordings may be copied freely from master copies in the Southeast Asia Section of the Library of Congress or from U.S.I.S. Bangkok.)

Mosel, James N. *Trends and Structure in Contemporary Thai Poetry.* Ithaca: Cornell University, Southeast Asia Program, Data Paper No. 43, 1961. 53 pages.

The revision of a paper presented in *United Asia,* Vol. XII, No. 2 (1960). States that "Serious literature in Thailand is almost exclusively equated with poetry;" contrasts traditional and contemporary Thai poetic forms and cites changing social conditions in Thailand as a major determinant of changing poetic style and form. One of the very few serious studies in the English language on the poetry of a Southeast Asian country. A series of Thai poems with translations and descriptive commentary is included.

Mueller, F. Max (trans.). *The Dhammapada: A Collection of Verses Being One of the Canonical Books of the Buddhists.* Vol. X in F. Max Mueller (ed.), *Sacred Books of the East,*

Second edition, revised. Oxford: Oxford University Press, 1924. 99 pages.

A translation of the Dhammapada from the Pali into English.

Purachatra, Prince Prem. *The Story of Phra Abhai Mani.* Bangkok: Chatra Books, 1952. 141 pages.

Sunthorn Bhu's classic Siamese tale told in English. A selection from this work can be found in *Orient Review and Literary Digest,* (Calcutta), August, 1956, pp. 82-111.

Schweisguth, P. *Étude sur la Littérature Siamoise.* Paris: Imprimerie Nationale de Paris, d'Amerique et d'Orient, 1951. 409 pages.

A ranging, historically organized survey of Thai literature, beginning with the era of Ramkamheng (1277-1317) and ending with a consideration of authors of the contemporary era. One chapter on the works of Prince Damrong. Includes a summary bibliography of Thai and Western sources for the study of Thai literature, an index of the volumes of the publication *Wachiryin,* a listing of sources of Ramakien poetry, and a list of printed versions of traditional Thai legends and folk tales. Authors, poets, and particular works are described, with two or three paragraphs devoted to each item. Drama is also treated.

Sharto, H. L., Judith M. Jacob, and E. H. S. Simmonds. *Bibliography of Mon-Khmer and Tai Linguistics.* See Section H.

Sibunruang, J. Kasem. *Siamese Folk Tales.* Bangkok: Prasom's, 1098-2 Krungtep-Samutprakarn Road, Bangkapi, 1954. 88 pages.

Five well-known Thai folk tales, including one popular in the south of Thailand and another known in the Eastern and Northeastern regions. (In English.)

Thailand Culture Series. Bangkok: National Culture Institute. 1954-1956. Now issued by the Fine Arts Department, following abolition of the Ministry of Culture, this series includes the seventeen brief pamphlets dealing with various aspects of Thai culture. Each has been prepared by a Thai authority. Together, the pamphlets listed below comprise a ranging commentary on aspects of Thai society and its cultural heritage.

1. Phya Anuman Rajadhon, "The Culture of Thailand." Brief discussion of the historical and ecological sources of Thai religion, art, literature, music, and drama. 61 pages.

2. Phya Anuman Rajadhon, "A Brief Survey of Cultural

Thailand." Describes Thai art forms, including architecture, sculpture, painting, music, drama, and literature. 16 pages.

3. Phya Anuman Rajadhon, "Thai Literature and Swasdi Raksa." Brief summaries and analyses of selected examples of the major Thai literary forms, with special emphasis on "Swasdi Raksa" (the safeguarding of one's welfare).

4. Prof. Silpa Birasri, "Thai Architecture and Painting." Brief analyses of architectural forms found in Thai Buddhist temples. Also an illustrated section on the artistic peculiarities and subjects of Thai painting. 24 pages.

5. Phya Anuman Rajadhon. "Loy Krathong and Songkran Festival." Brief discussion of the nature, history, and meaning of Loy Krathong (the floating of light in a leaf cup) and songkran (the traditional Thai New Year). 24 pages.

6. Phya Anuman Rajadhon. "Chao Thi and Some Traditions of Thai." A discussion of the rituals associated with Chao Thi (Phra Phum, the guardian spirit of the house), followed by a short treatment of the tradition associated with the "Khuan" (an attendant spirit residing within every individual). 15 pages.

7. Phya Anuman Rajadhon. "Pra Chedi." History and architectural analysis of the three types of Chedi (a sacred monument or reliquary). 12 pages.

8. Phra Chen Duriyanga. "Thai Music." Semi-technical discussion of Thai music; a description of the character and instrumental technique of Thai music; and examples of traditional Thai music with Western notation. 56 pages.

9. Luang Boribal Buribhand. "Thai Images of the Buddha." Short history of Thai images of the Buddha indicating the sources and unique features of each particular style. 12 pages.

10. Professor Silpa Birasri. "Thai Buddhist Sculpture." Illustrations, characterizations, and historical sketches of styles typical in the Chiengsen, Sukhothai, Uthong, Ayuthia, and Bangkok periods. 28 pages.

11. Prince Dhaninivat Kromamun Bidyalabh Bridhyakorn and Dhanit Yupho. "The Khon." Describes the Khon (Masked Play) in terms of content and technique, with colored illustrations and diagrams. 16 pages.

12. H. H. Prince Dhaninivat Kromamun Bidyalabh Bridhyakorn. "The Nang." The Nang (Shadow Play) described in terms of its origins accessories, techniques and stories. 16 pages.

13. Phya Anuman Rajadhon. "The Story of Thai Marriage Customs." Discusses Thai expressions, attitudes, and customs relating to marriage; depicts the events of the wedding

day and the particulars of the marriage ceremony. 16 pages.

14. Prof. Silpa Birasri. "Modern Art in Thailand." Sets out to "state the principal factors which determined the decline of the classic Thai art and the recent revival of art with modern characteristics." 12 pages.

15. Dhanit Yupho. "The Preliminary Course of Training in Thai Theatrical Art." Contains nine musical scores in Western notation, three versions of the "Alphabet of Thai Dancing," and illustrations of the comprehensive list of sixty-eight figures which form the alphabet. 64 pages.

16. Witt Siwasariyanon. "Life in Bangkok." Sketchy and dated collection of facts and figures about Bangkok. Describes places of interest to the foreign visitor. 16 pages.

17. Phya Anuman Rajadhon. "Thai Language." Describes the nature, roots, and development of the Thai language and alphabet. Contains charts of five alphabets used from A.D. 183-1660, charts of two current alphabets, and one map. 32 pages.

Urquhart, W. A. M. *Tales from Old Siam.* Bangkok: Progress Publishing Company, n.d. (1963). 155 pages.

Relates about twenty Thai folk tales, with a brief introduction by Phya Anuman Rajadhon. Appendix points out similarities between individual tales and the legends and stories found in other cultures and links the tales to Thai cultural motifs.

4. Minorities: Chinese, Muslims, Thai-Lao, and Hill Tribes

Burling, Robbins. *Hill Farms and Paddy Fields: Life in Mainland Southeast Asia.* See Section A.

Charusathira, General Praphas. "Thailand's Hill Tribes." *Thai Journal of Public Administration,* January, 1966, pp. 429-438.

Published under the authorship of the Thai Deputy Prime Minister and Minister of Interior. Considers the significance of tribal peoples to the nation's security; discusses the opium problem, questions of tribal citizenship, land rights, and permanent settlement of tribal peoples. Also acknowledges governmental responsibility for tribal welfare and presents a discerning and sensible statement of Thai government posture toward the hill tribes.

Coughlin, Richard J. *Double Identity: The Chinese in Modern Thailand*. Hong Kong: Hong Kong University Press (with Oxford University Press), 1960. 222 pages.

Briefer than Skinner's monumental work and Purcell's ranging study, and more limited in scope and content, but a useful introduction to the subject of the Chinese in Thailand.

Dibble, Charles R. "The Chinese in Thailand Against the Background of Chinese-Thai Relations." Unpublished Ph.D. dissertation, Syracuse University, 1961. 546 pages.

Concludes that contemporary Sino-Thais are essentially detached from any significant tendency to identify with either of the "two Chinas," and are increasingly oriented toward identification as Thai citizens. Includes an extensive bibliography.

Embree, John F., and William L. Thomas, Jr. *Ethnic Map and Gazetteer of Northern Southeast Asia*. See Section A.

Fraser, Thomas M., Jr. *Fishermen of South Thailand: The Malay Villagers*. See Section C-5.

Fraser, Thomas M., Jr. *Rusembilan: A Malay Fishing Village in Southern Thailand*. See Section C-5.

Hanks, Lucien M., J. R. Hanks, and Lauriston Sharp (eds.). *Ethnographic Notes on Northern Thailand*. Ithaca: Cornell University, Southeast Asia Program, Data Paper No. 58, 1965. 96 pages.

An interesting collection of twelve papers on aspects of the life of a small number of the many and varied tribal communities (including the Miao, Lahu, Yao, and the Lisu) in northern Thailand.

Hinton, Peter (ed.). *Tribesmen and Peasants in Northern Thailand*. Chiengmai: Tribal Research Centre, 1969.

A collection of papers presented to "The First Symposium on Hill-Tribes and Thailand" at the Tribal Research Centre in Chiengmai, August 28-September 1, 1967. Among the contributions is a statement of government policy regarding the tribal peoples in Thailand by Mr. Suwan Ruenyote, Director-General, Department of Public Welfare; reports of anthropological research on various tribal groups by R. W. Kickert (Akha), A. R. Walker (Red Lahu), D. J. Miles (Yao), P. Kunstradter (Lawa and

Karen), and D. Marlowe (Karen); reports of linguistic research on several tribal groups by D. Dellinger and P. Wyss (Akha) and D. H. Roop (Lisu); reports of anthropological research on Northern Thai peasants by G. Marlowe, K. Kingshill, and L. C. Judd; and comments by other researchers working on anthropological or linguistic studies in northern Thailand. The editor, an Australian anthropologist, provides a general summary statement of the implications of social research in northern Thailand, with particular emphasis on the tribal peoples.

Hunter, Guy. *South-East Asia: Race, Culture, and Nation.* London: Oxford University Press, 1966. 190 pages.

Written for the lay reader rather than the specialist, this is a good statement of the special ethnic, racial, and language problems that confront the developing nations of Southeast Asia.

Judd, Lawrence C. *Dry Rice Agriculture in Northern Thailand.* See Section E-1.

Keyes, Charles F. "Ethnic Identity and Loyalty of Villagers in Northeast Thailand." See Section G-1.

Keyes, Charles F. *Isan: Regionalism in Northeastern Thailand.* See Section G-1.

Keyes, Charles F. "Peasant and Nation: Thai-Lao Village in a Thai State." See Section C-5.

Kuhn, Isabel. *Ascent to the Tribes: Pioneering in North Thailand* (A China Mission Book). Chicago: Moody Press, 1956. 315 pages.

An account of the personal experience of a China Inland Mission worker in North Thailand, with comments on the political and cultural setting.

Kunstradter, Peter. *The Lua of Northern Thailand: Aspects of Social Structure, Agriculture, and Religion.* Princeton: Princeton University Center of International Studies, 1965. 56 pages.

Findings of fieldwork, 1963-1965, in Chiengmai and Maehongson Provinces, including the product of a three-month ethnographic study in one Lua village, Ban Pa Pae. Perhaps ten thousand Lua live in the northern Thailand mountains and thousands more are in various stages of assimilation into a broader Thai culture. A number of general observations concerning history and tradition are included.

Kunstradter, Peter (ed.). *Southeast Asian Tribes, Minorities and Nations*. 2 vols. Princeton: Princeton University Press, 1967. 902 pages.

Seven papers in this two-volume work are on Thailand. Four deal with specific Thai ethnic groups: Michael Moerman on Thai-Lue views of the central government; F.W. Mote on Haw (Yunnanese Chinese) immigrants as agents of social change; Peter Kandre on Yao (Iu Mien) social systems and relations with outsiders; and Peter Kunstradter on Lua and Karen adaptation to hill and valley life. Three papers (by Lee W. Huff, Hans Manndorff, and William R. Geddes) outline Thai governmental policies and programs dealing with these ethnic minorities. An introductory chapter by Kunstradter and chapter bibliographies provide very useful information concerning sources of research material.

Landon, Kenneth P. *The Chinese in Thailand*. London: Oxford University Press, 1941. 310 pages.

This book is of supplemental value for historical information and firsthand observations.

Lebar, Frank M., Gerald C. Hickey, John K. Musgrave, *et al. Ethnic Groups of Mainland Southeast Asia*. New Haven: Human Relations Area Files Press, 1964. 288 pages.

A ranging ethnographic description of the people of mainland Southeast Asia and the culturally related regions of southern China. The order of presentation is in terms of major language stocks (Sino-Tibetan, Austro-Asiatic, Tai-Kadai, Malayo-Polynesian). Within this general framework, distinctions are made between lowland and upland groups.

le May, Reginald S. *An Asian Arcady: The Land and People of Northern Siam*. See Section G-1.

Moerman, Michael. *Agricultural Change and Peasant Choice in a Thai Village*. See Section E-1.

Moerman, Michael. "Kinship and Commerce in a Thai-Lue Village." See Section G-1.

Northeasterners in the Chiengrai Area. See Section G-5.

Poole, Peter A. "Thailand's Vietnamese Minority." *Asian Survey*, December, 1967, pp. 886-895.

The story of Vietnamese refugees who fled from the French into Thailand, and of the some forty thousand who still remain in Thailand, much to the distress of the Thai government.

Purcell, Victor. *The Chinese in Southeast Asia.* London: Oxford University Press, 1965. 624 pages.

A new edition of an important work originally published in 1951; updated with an outline of events between 1949 and 1963, bibliographical additions, and other supplemental material. Part III, "The Chinese in Siam," is a relevant and extensive statement.

Report of the United Nations Survey Team on the Economic and Social Needs of the Opium-Producing Areas in Thailand. Bangkok: Government House Printing Office, vii, 1967, 114 pages + maps and photographs.

Draws both on the existing surveys of socio-economic conditions of tribal peoples in Thailand made by the Thai government in 1962 and again in 1965-66, and upon firsthand observations obtained by members of the survey team. The best summary of what is known about the whole of the tribal population of the kingdom. Also provides an assessment of the nature of the "opium problem" in Thailand and includes a set of recommendations concerning how this problem might be eliminated.

Report on the Socio-Economic Survey of the Hill Tribes in Northern Thailand. Bangkok: Department of Public Welfare, Ministry of the Interior, 1962.

An important report, as it represents the first attempt by the Thai government to gather information on the socio-economic conditions of Thailand's tribal population. Also provides some solid information on the distribution and characteristics of various tribal groups, offering a counterpoint to the impressionistic survey by Young, cited below.

Saihoo, Patya. "The Hill Tribes of Northern Thailand and the Opium Problem." *Bulletin on Narcotics,* Vol. 15, 1963, pp. 35-45.

A short statement of the character of the "opium problem" in Thailand by a Thai anthropologist who was involved in the Thai Government's 1962 study of tribal conditions.

Skinner, William G. *Chinese Society in Thailand: An Analytical History.* Ithaca: Cornell University Press, 1957. 459 pages.

A comprehensive historical analysis of the Chinese in Thailand. Authoritative and extraordinarily well-written, this is a definitive work on the subject.

Skinner, William G. *Leadership and Power in the Chinese Com-*

munity in Thailand. Ithaca: Cornell University Press, 1958. 363 pages.

Systematic descriptions of the structure of leadership in the Chinese community in Thailand, with particular emphasis on Bangkok. Valuable examination of relationships between Thai and Chinese leaders.

Strisavasdi, Boon Chuey. *The Hill Tribes of Siam.* Bangkok: Khun Aroon, 1963. 203 pages + 568 photographs.

Not a systematic or penetrating study, but a vivid volume, full of details about hill tribe life. Strisavasdi traveled widely collecting information and photographs presented in this pictorial essay.

"Symposium on Northeast Thailand." *Asian Survey,* July, 1966, pp. 349-380.

Short papers on Northeast Thailand first presented at the 1966 annual meeting of the Association for Asian Studies. The papers and comments are by David A. Wilson, David K. Wyatt, Millard F. Long, Charles F. Keyes, A. Thomas Kirsch, and William J. Gedney.

Thomas, M. Ladd. "Political Socialization of the Thai-Islam," in Robert Sakai (ed.), *Studies on Asia.* Lincoln: University of Nebraska Press, 1967, pp. 89-105.

Outlines efforts of the Thai government to deal with about seven hundred thousand Thai citizens of Malay stock in South Thailand. Describes the posture of the Malaysian communist terrorists toward this group, as well as the policy responses of the Thai government and the problems involved in efforts to implement them.

Thomas, M. Ladd. *Socio-Economic Approach to Political Integration of the Thai-Islam: An Appraisal.* See Section C-1.

Thompson, Virginia, and Richard Adloff. *Minority Problems in Southeast Asia.* Stanford: Stanford University Press, 1955. 295 pages.

Descriptions of various minorities in Southeast Asia and discussions of their social and economic circumstances. Includes material on Malays of southern Thailand.

Van Roy, Edward. "Economic Dualism and Economic Change Among the Hill Tribes of Thailand." *Pacific Viewpoint,* September, 1966, pp. 151-168.

An examination of the economy of the Sino-Tibetian tribes (Akha, Lahu, Lisu, Miao, and Yao) of North Thailand, particularly with respect to the problems their way of life poses to the Thai nation. Two tribal villages that have reacted differently to the encroachments of lowland civilization serve as cases in point.

Young, Gordon. *The Hill Tribes of Northern Thailand.* Bangkok: The Siam Society, 1962. 92 pages.

The socio-ethnological study of twenty hill tribe groups whose two hundred thousand members comprise significant (and strategically located) elements of Thailand's populace. Information on racial affiliations, populations, residence sites, language, religion, settlement and governmental patterns, economy, social customs, and social trends for each tribal group. The author, an honorary chief of the Lahu tribe, writes from unique personal knowledge.

5. Population

Caldwell, J. C. "The Demographic Structure," in T. H. Silcock (ed.), *Thailand: Social and Economic Studies in Development.* Canberra: Australian National University Press, 1967, pp. 27-64.

One of the few really good statements about the Thai demographic structure from the nineteenth century to the present. Concludes that there have been two modal points in Thailand's population history: the late nineteenth-century opening of the external market for rice sales and the period of rapidly decreasing mortality rates after World War II.

Gille, Halvor. "The Demographic Outlook of Thailand and Some Implications." Bangkok: National Seminar on the Population of Thailand, March 1963. 34 pages.

The revised version of a statement made at a conference sponsored by the National Research Council, government of Thailand, with the cooperation of the Population Council of New York City. Includes population projections based in part upon the 1960 census.

McCusker, Henry F. "The Relationship between Population and Social Development of Thailand." *Social Science Review* (Bangkok), June-August, 1967.

Discusses the effects of rapid population growth on education, social welfare expenditures, the rice balance, per capita income, and the supply of agricultural land. Concludes that the long-term growth of the Thai economy is likely to be seriously damaged by high population growth. Disputes also the "standard" cultural, military, and political objections to family planning.

Northeasterners in the Chiengrai Area. Bangkok: U.S. Agency for International Development, July, 1966. 10 pages + maps.

Discusses the northeasterners' migration into the northern region. Attempts to determine the reasons for migration and the attitudes of northern villagers toward the migrants. Economic activities of the migrants are also surveyed.

Report of the Asian Population Conference and Selected Papers. See Section A.

Report on the Research of the Problem of Thailand's Population Increase. Bangkok: National Research Council, 1963. 35 pages.

Discusses population theories and problems in various countries. A short chapter on the population of Thailand. 1910-1960.

Sternstein, L. "A Critique of Thai Population Data." *Pacific Review,* Vol. 6, No. 1, pp. 15-38.

Not examined.

Thailand Population Census. See Section E-4.

H.
BIBLIOGRAPHIES AND RELATED ITEMS

The coverage of the following bibliographies extends beyond the scope of the work at hand. Certain items that are not bibliographies in the technical sense of the word are also included.

Academic Advisory Council for Thailand. *Some Bibliographical Resources on Development in Thailand*. Los Angeles: University of California, 1970; 45 pages.

Identifies about eight hundred reports and other documents in several collections, including the Agency for International Development Reference Center, Washington, D.C.; the International Monetary Fund Reference Center, Washington, D.C.; the American University Center for Research in Social Systems; the Army's Engineer Agency for Resource Inventories, Washington; and the AACT Holdings at UCLA. The latter include many USOM/Thailand research reports. Items are not annotated, and entries are alphabetical within each organizational category. Compiled by Michael N. O'Hara, this preliminary survey of certain special collections also contains information about the conditions of access to each of them.

Amyot, Jacques. *Changing Patterns of Social Structure in Thailand: An Annotated Bibliography with Comments*. Delhi: UNESCO Research Center, 1965. 171 pages.

Cited in Amara Raksasataya, *Thailand: Social Science Materials in Thai and Western Languages*. Not examined.

Anglemyer, Mary, Janet G. Gee, and Michael G. Koll, Jr. *Selected Bibliography, Lower Mekong Basin*. Washington, D.C.: Engineer Agency for Resources Inventory, Department of the Army, June 15, 1969. 2 vols., 293 pages, 222 pages (loose-leaf).

Volume I deals with the Lower Mekong Basin region as a whole and with Thailand; volume II, with Cambodia, Laos, and Vietnam. These sections are, in turn, subdivided by subject matter: agriculture, climate, education, electric power, fisheries, forestry and vegetation, geology, health, industry, minerals, population, and soils. For the most part, the entries represent material available in the Washington, D.C. area. Entries are not annotated. (In English and French.)

Annotated Bibliography of Northeast Thailand. Bangkok: Joint Thai-U.S. Research and Development Center, 1967. 38 pages.

The 106 entries in this bibliography on Northeast Thailand range from elephant hunting to the story of a Northeast Siamese girlhood. Most, however, are of a technical nature, having to do with soil, water, topography, irrigation, transportation, and so on. Sequel to an earlier "exploratory" bibliography published by the Military Research and Development Center. All items are annotated.

Asia Research Bulletin. Singapore: *Straits Times Press*, published monthly. 76 pages.

Contains material from Thai, English, Chinese, and Malay newspapers, journals, and official publications, along with topical background pieces and statistical data. Cross referenced and indexed. Annual subscription (airmail to U.S.) $112.

Asia: A Guide to Paperbacks. Revised edition. New York: The Asia Society, 1968. 178 pages.

Few of the approximately 173 Southeast Asia entries are directly concerned with Thailand. Well annotated.

Asian Bibliography. Bangkok: Economic Commission for Asia and the Far East. Published semi-annually.

Issued in June and December of each year since 1952, this is actually the accessions list of the ECAFE library. Indexed by area; items are classified by topic. Non-English titles are translated into English. The scope and relevance of the ECAFE library's collection make this a useful source.

Bernath, Frances A. *Catalog of Thai Language Holdings in the Cornell University Libraries Through 1964.* Ithaca: Cornell University, Southeast Asia Program, Data Paper No. 54, December, 1964. 236 pages.

A reproduction of about five thousand catalog cards, arranged alphabetically by author or equivalent. This publication facilitates access to the leading collection of Thai materials to be found in an American university. Includes several hundred official reports and government publications — laws, judicial reports, and ministerial and departmental documents.

Berton, Peter, Alvin Z. Rubenstein, and Anna Allott. *Soviet Works on Southeast Asia: A Bibliography of Non-Periodical*

Literature, 1946-1965. Los Angeles: University of Southern California Press, 1967.

Only 20 of the 401 entries pertain directly to Thailand (54 to the general region), but the essay on Soviet Southeast Asian studies by Anna Allott is a worthwhile addition.

Bibliography: Cases and Other Materials for the Teaching of Business Administration in Developing Countries, South and Southeast Asia. Soldiers Field, Boston: Harvard University Graduate School of Business Administration, May, 1968. 408 pages.

Contains annotations of 653 cases, including six Thai cases, and brief annotations on some two hundred articles and four hundred books. Copies of the cases are available from the Intercollegiate Case Clearing House.

Bibliography of Material about Thailand in Western Languages. Bangkok: Central Library, Chulalongkorn University, 1960. 326 pages.

The first extensive bibliography compiled in Thailand of materials about Thailand in Western languages. Broad coverage of about five thousand items arranged under twenty topical headings. Includes a list of more than one hundred and fifty Western-language periodicals publishing occasional articles about Thailand. Not annotated.

Bibliography of Materials relating to Thailand, and Project Personnel. Ithaca: Cornell University, Thailand Project, 1967. 40 pages.

List of more than 250 publications of the staff, students, and associates of Cornell's Thailand Project covering the period 1947-1967. Includes a brief history of the project.

Bitz, Ira. *A Bibliography of English-Language Source Materials on Thailand in the Humanities, Social Sciences and Physical Sciences*. Washington, D.C.: Social Science Research Institute. Distributed by the Clearinghouse for Federal Scientific and Technical Information, Bureau of Standards, U.S. Department of Commerce, June 1968. 271 pages.

The items are divided into sections on the basis of a modified version of the Human Relations Area Files' *Outline of Cultural Materials*. The aim of this bibliography is to be comprehensive rather than qualitatively selective. Some of the "better" items are briefly annotated.

A Compilation of Reports and Publications. Bangkok: U.S. Agency for International Development, 1965. 95 pages.

A bibliography of Bangkok-AID technical reports and publications deemed to be of "current interest or substantial research value." Covers material issued through the first quarter of 1964. Eleven functional categories: agricultural development, communications media, terminal assignment reports, education and human resources, investment opportunities, public administration, public safety, internal security and civic action, public works and engineering, social development, and Thai-American economic cooperation. See also USOM-Thailand Technical Library, this section.

Cormack, Margaret L. *Guidelines for South and Southeast Asia Resources in the U.S.* Berkeley: University of California, Center for South/Southeast Asia Studies, 1969.
Not examined.

Embree, John F., and Lillian Ota Dotson. *Bibliography of the Peoples and Cultures of Mainland Southeast Asia.* New Haven: Yale University, Southeast Asia Studies, 1950. 821 pages + addendum.
Pages 461-558 of this monumental compilation deal with Thailand and the Thai people. "No attempt is made to include political history, economics or welfare although all of these fields are partially included in various contexts. Human geography is largely included in the ethnology sections and some material on education is included under cultural history" (p. xiv). A valuable tool for social and cultural research.

External Research: A List of Recently Completed Studies; Southeast Asia and Southwest Pacific. (ER List No. 3.19). Washington: Department of State, Bureau of Intelligence and Research, External Research Staff. Published annually.
Issued each fall on the basis of information provided voluntarily by private scholars in the United States. Covers social science research, includes items completed even though in some cases not published, and identifies the academic affiliation of the scholar in each case. Items are not annotated. The External Research Staff also maintains an External Research Catalog, in which new projects are listed as information is received and research in progress is listed annually in the spring issues.

Gedney, William J. "Thailand and Laos." See Section G-3.

Hay, Stephen N., and Margaret H. Case (eds.). *Southeast Asian History: A Bibliographic Guide.* New York: Frederick A. Praeger, 1962. 132 pages.

An annotated bibliography of Southeast Asian history. Section I, pp. 89-100, comprises Thailand.

Henderson, Dan Fenno. *Bibliography of English-Language Materials on the Law of Thailand.* Seattle: University of Washington, School of Law, 1963. 12 pages.
Not examined.

Hobbs, Cecil (comp.). *Southeast Asia: An Annotated Bibliography of Selected Reference Sources in Western Languages.* Revised and enlarged edition. Washington, D.C.: Orientalia Division, Reference Department, Library of Congress, 1964. 180 pages.

This excellent work updates and extends an earlier (1952) compilation. Five hundred and thirty-five entries are included, mostly references to volumes published from 1942 through 1962. Full and carefully prepared annotations. Eighty-five citations to materials on Southeast Asia will be found, covering history, politics, economics, culture, and social conditions. Another fifty-three references cover the same terrain for Thailand. Most of the latter are also included within the work at hand. A new edition is in preparation.

Ichikawa, Kenjiro. *Southeast Asia Viewed from Japan: A Bibliography of Japanese Works on Southeast Asian Societies, 1940-1963.* Ithaca: Cornell University, Southeast Asia Program, Data Paper No. 56, 1965. 112 pages.

Printed in Japanese with translations of titles into English, this bibliography is unannotated.

International Political Science Abstracts. Oxford, England: Basil Blackwell. Published quarterly.

Prepared by the International Political Science Association in cooperation with the International Committee for Social Sciences Documentation, with support from UNESCO, this book provides annotations of materials in a large number of journals and other publications. The classification scheme enables identification and tentative evaluation of political science materials on Thailand.

Journal of Asian Studies. Published quarterly.

The *Journal,* published in the United States by the Association for Asian Studies, Inc., includes an annual bibliographical issue each September identifying by author and various categories books, articles, and some documents, reports, and dissertations on Asia, Asian regions, and Asian countries. Most materials covered are in English.

Journal of the Siam Society (JSS), Index to Volumes I to XXV. Bangkok: The Siam Society, 1935.

Journal of the Siam Society (JSS), Index to Volumes XXVI to XL. Bangkok: The Siam Society, 1955.

In addition to a general table of contents citing articles, book reviews, and notes on recent Thai publications, each index contains a classification of articles by author and by subject.

Konoshima, Sumiye. *Directory of Community Development Institutions in Asia.* Honolulu: East-West Center Library, University of Hawaii, Occasional Paper No. 3, 1965. 109 pages.

Eight pages (86-93) deal with the organization of the Thai Department of Community Development, including a listing of papers and memoranda produced by CD staff within the department.

Kozicki, Richard and Peter Ananda. *South and Southeast Asia: Doctoral Dissertations and Masters' Theses Completed at the University of California, Berkeley, 1906-1968.* Berkeley: University of California, Center for South/Southeast Asia Studies, 1969.

Not examined.

List of Scientific Reports Relating to Thailand. Bangkok: Thai National Documentation Centre, National Research Council, List No. 1, October, 1964. 126 pages.

Prepared by the Thai National Documentation Centre, which seeks to facilitate scientific research by making available information on investigations already undertaken. The TNDC will provide photocopies of reports shown on its list if the material is otherwise not available. The list itself consists of 1,263 individual items, cited by title and author, with source and language indicated. A title index is also included. The numbered items are arranged according to topic; the topics range from "Agriculture" through "Wood."

Mason, John Brown, and H. Carroll Parish. *Thailand Bibliography.* Gainesville: University of Florida Libraries, 1958. 247 pages.

Over two thousand three hundred references, many with brief annotations, including material in nine Western languages. The sheer scope of the work, coupled with minimal topical arrangement of materials and the absence of an index, make this bibliography difficult to use. One helpful feature is a list of Library of Congress holdings of English-language newspapers and periodicals published in Thailand, plus an identification of U.S. libraries at which some of these items are available.

McVey, Ruth T. *Bibliography of Soviet Publications on Southeast Asia.* Ithaca: Cornell University, Southeast Asia Program, Data Paper No. 34, 1959. 109 pages.

A bibliography based upon the Library of Congress Monthly Index of Russian acquisitions.

Nunn, G. Raymond. *South and Southeast Asia: A Bibliography of Bibliographies.* Honolulu: East-West Center Library, University of Hawaii, Occasional Paper No. 4, 1966. 59 pages.

Includes a listing of fifteen bibliographies on Southeast Asia and eleven on Thailand, classified by language of publication and publishing agency.

Public Administration Technicians' Reports: An Annotated Bibliography of Technicians' Reports on File Covering the Years 1959-1966. Washington, D.C.: U.S. Agency for International Development, Office of Technical Cooperation and Research, 1966. 74 pages.

Cites about seventy unclassified reports prepared by public administration direct-hire or contract technicians of AID for the years 1959-1966. Many are quarterly or semi-annual progress reports or end-of-tour reports. A few are substantive studies. Items are annotated, arranged by topic, and within topic by country.

Raksasataya, Amara, with Veeravat Kanchanadul, Prachak Suthayakom, *et al. Thailand: Social Science Materials in Thai and Western Languages.* Bangkok: The National Institute of Development Administration, 1966. 378 pages.

Pages 1-132 contain citations of Western-language materials, entered both by author and by title. Later sections also identify a number of Western-language bibliographies and Western-language periodicals. Extensive citations of Thai materials classified by author or, if anonymous, by publisher. Not annotated, and uses only an alphabetical classification. (In English and Thai.)

Sharto, H. L., Judith M. Jacob, and E. H. S. Simmonds. *Bibliographies of Mon-Khmer and Tai Linguistics.* London Oriental Bibliographies. Volume 2. London: Oxford University Press, 1963. 87 pages.

The Mon-Khmer bibliography lists all known works on languages of the group published up to 1961. The Tai bibliography covers work through 1959, with some later entries. Section II of the Tai bibliography contains 223 citations to general works, dictionaries, grammars, readers, and specialized linguistic studies.

Shimaoka, Helene R. (comp.). *Selected Bibliographies on Labor and Industrial Relations in Burma, Indonesia, Korea, Malaya, Singapore, Thailand.* Honolulu: Industrial Relations Center, University of Hawaii, 1961. 62 pages.

Lists seventy-nine items on Thailand. Not annotated.

Starbird, Ann, Sasinee Jotikasthere, and Surang Kongset. *Annotated Bibliography of Northeast Thailand.* Bangkok: Joint Thai-U.S. Military Research and Development Center, July, 1967. 38 pages.

Includes bibliographic data and brief annotation of 106 reports, monographs, and journal articles. Surveys the geographical, political, cultural, social, and economic aspects of Northeast Thailand.

Statistical Bibliography: An Annotated Bibliography of Thai Government Statistical Publications. Second edition. Bangkok: National Statistical Office, 1964. 175 pages.

Cites 165 Thai government statistical publications, annotated in both Thai and English, with indication of the language used in each report. Identifies sources of statistics on economic development, agriculture, communications, defense, education, finance, health, industry, and justice. A comparison of the first and second editions reflects a rapid growth in the collection and production of various kinds of statistical data, which is interesting and significant.

Stucki, Curtis W. *American Doctoral Dissertations on Asia, 1933-1962.* Ithaca: Cornell University, Southeast Asia Program, Data Paper No. 50, 1963. 204 pages.

Includes citations of eighty dissertations on Thailand, fourteen of which were produced at Cornell (at least five of the latter have been published). An appendix lists Master's theses on Asia submitted at Cornell during the period covered. Citations are not annotated.

The, Lian, and Paul W. van der Veur. *Treasures and Trivia: Doctoral Dissertations on Southeast Asia Accepted by Universities in the United States.* Athens, Ohio: Center for International Studies, Southeast Asia Program, Ohio University, 1968. 141 pages.

Lists doctoral dissertations on Southeast Asia done in

American universities, 136 of them on Thailand. The earliest entries are dated prior to the 1930's, and the most recent, mid-1968. Items are not annotated.

The University of Chicago Doctoral Dissertations and Master's Theses on Asia, 1894-1962. Chicago: Far Eastern Library, University of Chicago, 1962.

Not examined.

USOM-Thailand Technical Library: Document Section Card Catalog. Bangkok: U.S. Agency for International Development, 1967. 580 pages.

The cards reproduced in this catalog represent the complete holdings of the Document Section of the Bangkok-AID library, as of December 31, 1967. Not all of these materials are of AID origin, and many are not concerned with Thai subjects.

Wainwright, M. D., and Noel Matthews. *A Guide to Western Manuscripts and Documents in the British Isles Relating to South and Southeast Asia.* London: Oxford University Press, 1965. 532 pages.

Contains material found in the British Isles, dating from 1450, including the entire collection in the India Office Library. Items are briefly but adequately identified.

Wyatt, David. *Preliminary Checklist of Thailand Serials.* Ithaca: Cornell University, Thailand Project, 1971.

A preliminary listing of all serials concerning Thailand known to have been published inside or outside Thailand, in all languages, with notations on major United States holdings. Covers materials from about 1840, and draws upon prior work covering the serial literature through 1930. Monumental and thoroughly valuable.

Wyatt, David K., and Constance M. Wilson. "Thai Historical Materials in Bangkok." See Section B-1.

I.
OTHER SOURCES OF INFORMATION

No one has managed to produce a bibliography anticipating future scholarship. We can, however, identify sources of data and places of appearance for forthcoming literature on Thailand. This section notes a series of organizations of special importance to the Thai scholar, either because they serve as data repositories, or because they engage in the production of studies, or both. Also identified are newspapers and periodicals of value for the Western-language scholar, along with a source of access to them. Finally, certain periodically-issued directories and related sources of relevant material are noted.

1. Academic Programs

The study of the countries of Southeast Asia in the United States owes a great deal to the pioneering work of such scholars as John F. Embree of Yale and Lauriston Sharp of Cornell. In 1947 Yale's *Southeast Asia Studies Center* became the country's first center for the concerted interdisciplinary study of the peoples and cultures of Southeast Asia. Notable, too, is the Cornell University *Southeast Asia Program*. Cornell has published studies of Thai subjects at intervals since 1951, some of them of great value.

The University of Michigan *Center for South and Southeast Asian Studies* has the most comprehensive program and probably the most extensive Southeast Asian library collection in the Midwest. At least two other midwestern universities also have Southeast Asia programs — Northern Illinois, with a well-established *Center for Southeast Asian Studies,* and Ohio University, with its *Southeast Asian Program* established within the *Center for International Studies* in the fall of 1967.

On the West Coast, there are at least two notable Southeast

Asia programs: one within the *Center for South and Southeast Asian Studies* at the University of California, Berkeley; the other within the *Asian Studies Program* at the University of Washington. The University of California at Los Angeles has a *Thai-Lao Program*, a cluster of research and related activities concerning Thailand and Laos.

The long-established *School of African and Oriental Studies*, University of London, may still be the premier non-American center for Southeast Asian studies, although the *Center for Southeast Asian Studies* established at Kyoto University in 1963 has made an impressive mark, with studies of ranging variety. The Kyoto Center maintains a research office in Bangkok, supports field studies, and publishes materials in English as well as in Japanese. The Center's journal, *Tonan Ajia Kenkyu* (Southeast Asian Studies) is available in English translation from the Clearinghouse for Scientific and Technical Information, Springfield, Virginia 22151. Volumes I-IV of the journal include a number of sociological and anthropological studies of Thailand:

> Shigeru Iijima. "Culture change among the Hill Karens in Thailand," (II-4, pp. 2-19).
> Shigeru Iijima. "Plain emulation of Hill Karens in Northern Thailand," (III-5, pp. 40-71).
> Keiji Iwata. "Techniques of rice cultivation in Northern Thailand," (I-2, pp. 22-38).
> Keiji Iwata. "The process of disorganization and reorganization of rural society in Northern Thailand," (II-2, pp. 2-29).
> Koichi Mizuno. "The Don Deng Village," (II, pp. 112-119).
> Koichi Mizuno. "Land tenure and family in a rice-growing village in Northeast Thailand," (III-2, pp. 7-35).
> Koichi Mizuno. "Functional system of religious activities in a rice-growing village in Northeast Thailand," (III-3, pp. 2-21).
> Koichi Mizuno. "Don Deng Village, Thailand," (IV, pp. 194-201).
> Toru Yano. "A socio-anthropological survey in Songkhla province: a preliminary report," (III-1, pp. 140-143).
> Toru Yano. "Continuity and discontinuity of politics in Thailand," (I-1, pp. 31-43).
> Jikai Fujiyoshi. "An observation of the present situation of Thai Buddhism," (III-3, pp. 130-139).

Other Sources of Information 133

>Koji Sato. "On personality training through Satipatthana meditation in Burma, Thailand and Ceylon," (III-1, pp. 12-21).
>Iichi Sagara. "A comparative study of educational administrative organizations in Southeast Asian countries," (III-1, pp. 2-14).
>Takeshi Motooka. "Economic development and agriculture in Thailand," (III-5, pp. 2-39).
>Kasem Udyanin. "Development of Thai administration," (III-3, pp. 108-116).

Other studies reported in the journal, Volumes I-III, deal with the mining industry in Thailand and Malaysia, geology and ore deposits, geophysical prospecting, forest-crop estimates, soils and vegetation, crops, water resources, medicine and disease, and crude drugs.

2. Organizations and Other Data Sources

Academic Advisory Council for Thailand, University of California, 405 Hilgard Avenue, Los Angeles, California 90024. Professor David Wilson, Executive Secretary; Professor Lauriston Sharp, Chairman.

>AACT serves as an informal clearinghouse of information about scholars engaged in research concerning Thailand. The Council has issued a directory of scholars and their projects, identifying more than one hundred and fifty Thai, Japanese, European, and American scholars.

Advanced Research Projects Agency (ARPA), Bangkok, Thailand.

>ARPA is an element of the office of the U.S. Defense Department, sponsoring and conducting research in Thailand (both classified and unclassified). In cooperation with the Thai government, it has operated a Joint Thai-U.S. Military Research and Development Center in Bangkok, which has produced such materials as the *Annotated Bibliography of Northeast Thailand* noted in Section H. The Military Research and Development Center also operates the Thailand Information Center (TIC) described in this section.

Agency for International Development, Washington, D.C. and 642 Petchburi Road, Bangkok, Thailand.

AID is a substantial source of information, mostly in the form of reports written by AID personnel or under AID sponsorship. Bibliographies of materials available at either AID-Washington or AID-Bangkok, several of which are cited in Section H, are issued periodically.

AID-Bangkok also has on file a substantial number of mimeographed "in-house" research reports which, though not widely circulated, are nevertheless generally available on request. At intervals the Research Division has issued lists of its publications, one as recently as October, 1968. Some of the reports available through the Research Division include: "Current Research Projects in Thailand (1966)"; "Innovations in Ubol Changwad (1966)"; "USOM Programs in Sokol Nakorn (1966)"; "An Evaluation of the Home Guard by Local Officials, Members of the Guard and Villagers (1968)"; and "Field Interviews with Amphoe, Tambon and Muban Officials and Villagers About Local Administrators and Local Problems in Changwad Udorn Thani (1968)." Certain of these AID reports are cited elsewhere in this bibliography.

American Foundations in Bangkok

The following American-based foundations support developmental efforts in higher education, the social sciences, agriculture, the humanities, and medicine, while maintaining offices in Bangkok:

Asia Foundation (headquarters: San Francisco)
Agricultural Development Council (headquarters: New York)
Ford Foundation (headquarters: New York)
Rockefeller Foundation (headquarters: New York)

The Asia Society, Asia House, 112 East 64th Street, New York, New York 10020.

The Asia Society was founded in 1957 to spread knowledge of Asia among Americans. It provides information about Asia through lectures, conferences, and publications — including the quarterly journal *Asia*.

The Asian Institute for Economic Development and Planning, Sanam-ma Road, Bangkok, Thailand.

The Institute, a United Nations training and research facility, may be an excellent future source of economic data and related matters. It was established in 1964 by the U.N. Special Fund and the ECAFE countries to serve the ECAFE region.

Association of Southeast Asian Institutions of Higher Learning,

Ratasastra Building, Chulalongkorn University, Henri Dunant Road, Bangkok, Thailand. Prince Prem Purachatra, Executive Secretary.

The Association has published a handbook (see Section F-1) describing institutions of higher learning in Southeast Asia. It also publishes selected papers given at various conferences and seminars. Member institutions exist in eight countries: Thailand, Burma, Hong Kong, Indonesia, Malaysia, Philippines, Singapore, and Vietnam.

Business Research, Ltd., Rajprasong Road, Bangkok, Thailand.

In 1967 this was one private organization engaged in survey research. By 1969 at least two other such organizations were known to be active in Thailand.

Council of Social Science Data Archives, Bureau of Applied Social Research, 605 West 115th Street, New York, New York 10025.

The Council maintains information on specialized archives and social science information services, and may be of use to scholars seeking Thai data sources.

National Institute of Development Administration, Klong Jan, Bangkok, Thailand.

The Institute's quarterly *Journal of Development Administration* includes occasional articles in English, a bilingual table of contents, and English-language abstracts of articles and Master's theses submitted to the Institute. The research division and library of the Institute are useful sources of information on Thai government documents and reports. (NIDA absorbed the Thai Institute of Public Administration, Thammasat University, in April, 1966. The new journal is an expanded, retitled version of the *Thai Journal of Public Administration,* published quarterly from 1960-1966.)

ECAFE (Economic Commission for Asia and the Far East), Sala Santitham, Bangkok 2, Thailand, and other *United Nations* organizations.

A source of commentary and data on regional and country economic and related matters. A reference to the semi-annual ECAFE *Asian Bibliography* is located in Section H. The Commission published annually the comprehensive *Economic Survey of Asia and the Far East,* and quarterly the *Economic Bulletin for Asia and the Far East.* Other United Nations organizations with offices in Bangkok are the following: UNESCO, UNTAB, Special Fund, FAO, ICAO, ILO, UNICEF, WHO, World Bank, and the Committee for Coordination of Investigation of the Lower Mekong Basin. *The United Nations in Thailand: A Brief Account of the Activities of the United Nations and the Specialized Agencies in Thailand,* 1968 (52 pages), is available without charge from ECAFE.

Institute of Southeast Asian Studies, Cluny Road, Singapore 10.

The Institute of Southeast Asian Studies in currently building a highly qualified staff with a view to becoming a major research center in Southeast Asia. Current activities, however, do not include an intensive focus upon Thailand.

National Research Council, Office of the Prime Minister, Bangkok, Thailand.

Established to promote and encourage research in the natural and social sciences, the Council serves as a clearinghouse and subsidizes certain kinds of studies. It issued a *Directory of Natural Scientific Institutions in Thailand,* 1964 (10 pages), listing sixty-four institutions engaged in various types of natural science research. The Council also issued a *Directory of Natural and Social Scientific Institutions in Thailand,* 1963 (16 pages), identifying various organizations claiming to be engaged in one or another type of social science research. In 1964 the NRC published the first issue of a *List of Scientific Reports Relating to Thailand* (see Section H). The NRC also attempts to maintain a register of research in progress.

Research Publications, Publishers in the Microfilms, 254 College Street, New Haven, Connecticut.

Research Publications makes available copies of certain Asian periodicals in either microfilm or xerox copy, at moderate prices. Thai materials available from Research Publications include: the *Journal of the Siam Society,* 1904-1964; the *Bangkok Calendar,* 1857-1873; the *Bangkok World,* 1957-1964; and the *Siam Rath Weekly Review,* 1954-1964.

SEATO (Southeast Asia Treaty Organization), P.O. Box 517, Bangkok, Thailand.

SEATO publishes the bimonthly *SEATO Record,* containing brief items about SEATO and its member countries, and statements reflecting SEATO policies. Information on SEATO development projects in Thailand is included.

The Siam Society, 131 Lane 21, (Asoka), Sunhumvit Road, Bangkok, Thailand.

The Siam Society was founded in 1904, for the "investigation and encouragement of Art, Science, and Literature in relation to Siam and neighboring countries." The more than forty volumes of *The Journal of the Siam Society*, with most articles in English, are and will continue to be a valuable source of scholarly work in history, archaeology, law, and other fields.

Social Science Association Press of Thailand, Phyathai Road, Bangkok, Thailand.

The Press publishes a *Social Science Review*, mostly in Thai. It also has issued about a dozen volumes of work by Thai scholars in Thai, and an English-language work, *The Economy of Thailand*, by André Mousny. The Social Science Association Press may become a useful source of Western-language material for scholars in the future.

Thailand Information Center, 518/4 Ploenchit Road, Bangkok.

TIC is a component of the Advanced Research Projects Agency (ARPA) Research and Development Center. It has been developing and operating a computerized information retrieval system, with inputs in the form of documents, some restricted and others not. Early in 1969, "locators" had been issued identifying numerically documents on file for provinces in the Northeast and for fourteen Southern provinces, and "locators" were being developed to identify collected documents covering North Thailand, the Central Region, and Hill Tribes and Ethnic Groups. The long-range aim of this information system is to establish monumental data collections on various Thai topics with quick access through computerized filing.

United Nations. See *ECAFE*, this section.

United States Information Service, Sathorn Road, Bangkok, Thailand.

USIS-Bangkok has conducted research at intervals since about 1959. A substantial number of unclassified studies, largely communication and media surveys, have been produced.

3. Directories

Amphoe-Tambon Statistical Directory of 14 ARD Changwads. See Section C-5.

Amyot, Jacques, and Robert W. Kickert (eds.). *Directory of the Social Sciences in Thailand*. Bangkok: The Faculty of Political Science, Chulalongkorn University, 1963. 100 pages.

Lists Thai and foreign social scientists in Thailand by name, discipline, area of research interest, and organizational affiliation — as of 1963.

Board of Trade Directory, 1967. See Section E-1.

Changwad-Amphoe Statistical Directory. See Section E-4.

Commercial Directory for Thailand. Bangkok: Department of Commercial Intelligence, Ministry of Economic Affairs. Issued irregularly.

Contains information on government organization, economic and commercial legislation, foreign trade, a complete customs schedule and an explanation of customs regulations, a brief directory of trade associations, manufacturers, and businesses. Not as attractive a production as the privately produced *Siam Directory.*

Directory of USOM Participants. Bangkok: U.S. Agency for International Development, 1965. 566 pages.

Lists more than three thousand two hundred Thai nationals who have studied abroad under AID sponsorship. Participants are listed by name, functional field of training or study, and province of their origin. In 1969 a new directory was in preparation.

Organizational Directory of the Government of Thailand. Bangkok: U.S. Agency for International Development, Public Administration Division, 1968-1969. 70 pages.

Issued periodically. Identifies all units of the Thai bureaucracy to the division level, as well as the officials in charge, providing a detailed English-language portrait of the formal organizational structure of the Thai bureaucracy.

Royal Thai Government Gazette. Edited by M. R. Tanaumsri Devakul. Bangkok: International Translations, New Road.

Issued weekly since 1946, this indexed translation of Thai laws, regulations, decrees, rulings, and significant personnel changes is the English-language source of information of official transactions of the Thai government. There are, of course, inevitable problems in the continuing translation of highly technical legal documents, and some care must be taken in the use of this unofficial English-language version of the *Government Gazette.*

SEADAG Directory, 1968-1969. New York: Southeast Asia Development Advisory Group, The Asia Society, 1969. 153 pages.

Compiled and edited by Avery Russell, the *Directory* identi-

Other Sources of Information 139

fies about two hundred and fifty individuals with scholarly and other professional interests in Southeast Asia, and provides information on their location, Southeast Asian experience, professional status, and publications. U.S. Government participants in SEADAG are identified in a separate section. The *Directory* also contains a list of forty-five papers prepared by SEADAG members, and a description of SEADAG aims and activities. Funded by AID, the organization was established under the aegis of The Asia Society to promote scholarly activity and communication between scholars and officials and among the different academic disciplines dealing with Southeast Asia.

The Siam Directory. Bangkok: Thai Company, 96 Mansion 2, Rajdamnern Avenue. $13 US.

A valuable reference, issued at intervals. A directory of Thai government organizations, business firms, a copy of the current Thai constitution, information on commerce, business regulations, the current economic development program, and dozens of other items are included.

Tilman, Robert O. (Project Director). *International Biographical Directory of Southeast Asia Specialists, 1969*. Inter-university Southeast Asia Committee of the Association of Asian Studies. Distributed by the Center for International Studies, Ohio University, 1969. 279 pages + indices.

Extensive biographical data, based on questionnaire response of one thousand Southeast Asian specialists. Includes an introductory essay by Tilman and Garry D. Brewer. Identifies 213 individuals (including 132 U.S. nationals) who listed Thailand as the first country of their specialization, and another 117 designating it as the second country of specialization. Twenty-six Thais are included.

4. Major Journals

Much of the current English-language writing about Thai government, politics, economics, and society is published in a relatively limited number of journals, including the following (except where noted, these journals are published in the United States):

Asian Survey
Eastern World (London)
Far Eastern Economic Review (Hong Kong)
Journal of Asian Studies
Journal of Developing Areas
Journal of Development Studies
Journal of Southeast Asian Studies (Singapore); before March 1970, the *Journal of Southeast Asian History*
Journal of the Siam Society (Bangkok)
Pacific Affairs

Relevant items have also appeared at times in such journals as *Administrative Science Quarterly, American Anthropologist, Asia, China Quarterly, Current History, The Economist, Foreign Affairs, International Development Review,* and *Journal of the American Oriental Society.*

5. English-Language Newspapers and Periodicals

Bangkok Bank Monthly Review, Bangkok Bank Ltd., 3-9 Suapa Road, Bangkok.
A specialized monthly newsletter of high quality.

Bangkok Post (daily), Mansion 4, Rajdamnern Avenue, Bangkok.
Strives within the constraints of political discretion for a good coverage of political and governmental events and personalities. Occasionally includes interpretive articles.

Bangkok World (daily), 522 Prasumaine Road, Bangkok.
The locally-owned *World*, though somewhat more circumspect than the *Post*, reports on the Thai political and government scene.

Foreign Affairs Bulletin (bimonthly), Bangkok: Department of Information, Thai Ministry of Foreign Affairs.
Published in English. Contains news and official comment on Thai foreign affairs and foreign policy.

The Investor (monthly), published for Thailand's Board of Investment by Siam Publications, Ltd., P.O. Box 2/150, Bangkok 2, Thailand.

A business and economic review that started publication in December, 1968, under the editorship of Dr. Amnuey Viravan. In addition to articles on trade and finance, contains current reports on law, economic development, and investment, and selected economic indicators. Judging from the first issue, *The Investor* promises to serve as a key source of current economic information.

Siam Rath (weekly), Mansion 6, Rajdamnern Avenue, Bangkok.
Edited by M. R. Kukrit Pramoj, a well-known Thai intellectual. Sometimes has editorials and features on matters of interest to the student of Thai government and politics, although it lacks the scope and coverage of the daily papers. Until the spring of 1966, when publication of the English-language edition ceased, it was one of two English-language weeklies in Bangkok.

The Standard (weekly), 77 Rama V Road, Bangkok.
Advertised as "a weekly newspaper for international readers," *The Standard* is the oldest active English-language newspaper in Bangkok. The scope of its news coverage is not so great as that of the dailies; occasionally, however, the *Standard* contains useful features and items about important Thai figures.

6. Booksellers

The Cellar Bookshop, 18090 Wyoming, Detroit, Michigan 48221.
Specializes in Southeast Asian materials and issues catalogs at irregular intervals.

Paragon Book Gallery, Ltd., 14 East 38th Street, New York City.
Issues an extensive catalog at intervals, apparently quarterly. For example, Catalog #41, Spring 1966, contains 218 citations of Southeast Asian materials, of which almost ten per cent concern Thailand.

Susil Gupta, Antiquarian Booksellers, 7A High Street, Wanstead, London E11.
At intervals issues catalogs of out-of-print and new books on Southeast Asia. Thus, Catalogue #52, n.d., contains more than sixteen hundred listings, including several dozen pertinent for the Thai scholar.

INDEX

Academic Advisory Council for Thailand, 122, 133
Adloff, Richard, 10, 119
Advanced Research Projects Agency (ARPA), 133
Alabaster, Henry, 104
Allott, Anna, 123
Amatayakul, Ravi, 59
American University, Special Operations Research Office, 10
Amyot, Jacques, 137
Andrews, James M., 60, 69
Anglemyer, Mary, 122
Angsusingha, Pakorn, 50
Anspach, Ralph, 6
Anuman Rajadhon, Phya, 92, 112, 113, 114
Arromdee, Virach, 68
Artamonoff, George L., 60
Asia Society, 123, 134
Asian Institute for Economic Development and Planning, 134
Askenasy, Alexander, R., 96
Association of Southeast Asian Institutions of Higher Learning, 85, 135
Association for Asian Studies, 127 (annot)
Atibaed, Sanee, 30
Attagara, Kingkeo, 104
Atthakor, Bunchana, 72
Ayal, Eliezer B., 6, 25, 69, 72

Bang, Nguyen Huu, 90
Bank of Thailand, 79, 80
Barbour, Ernest J., 55
Barry, Jean, 84
Behrman, Jere R., 60, 72
Bell, Peter, 73
Benda, Harry J., 2
Benedict, Ruth F., 92

Bernard, Henri, 20
Bernath, Frances A., 123
Berton, Peter, 123
Biehl, Max, 7
Birasri, Silpa, 113, 114
Biriyayodhin, Parayut, 61
Bitz, Ira, 124
Black, Eugene R., 2
Blakeslee, D. J., 32
Blanchard, Wendell, 2
Block, Edward Leigh, 33
Board of Investment of Thailand, 60
Board of Trade of Thailand, 61
Bone, Robert C., 2
Bowie, Theodore, 108
Bowring, Sir John, 13
Bradley, William L., 104
Brembeck, Cole S., 87
Brewer, Garry D., 139
Bridhyakorn, Prince Dhaninivat Kromamun Bidyalabh, 113
Brimmell, J. H., 33
Brown, James Marvin, 109
Brown, L. R., 73
Buasri, Thomrong, 86
Bunnag, Tej, 50
Buranasiri, Prayad, 73
Bureau of the Budget of Thailand, 51
Buribhand, Luang Boribal, 113
Burling, Robbins, 2
Burney, H., 19
Burtt, Edwin A., 104
Busch, Noel F., 3
Business Research, Ltd., 93, 135
Buss, Claude A., 3
Butwell, Richard, 3

Cady, John F., 3
Caldwell, J. C., 120
Campbell, Stuart, 109
Carter, A. Cecil, 13

Case, Margaret H., 125
Chakrabongse, Prince Chula, 13
Charusathira, Praphas, 114
Choisy, Abbè François Timoléon de, 13, 21(annot)
Chomchai, Prachoom, 13
Choosanay, Manoo, 55
Chu, Valentin, 3
Chulalongkorn University, 124
Clubb, Oliver E., Jr., 44
Coast, John, 25
Coedés, George, 4
Collis, Maurice, 20
Commercial Directory for Thailand, 138
Cornell University, Thailand Project, 124
Coughlin, Richard J., 115
Council of Social Science Data Archives, 135
Coward, H. Roberts, 33
Cowing, Susan Brown, 4(annot)
Crawfurd, John, 14
Credner, Wilhelm, 4
Cressey, George B., 4
Crosby, Josiah, 14
Crozier, Brian, 4
Cruagao, Paitoon, 92
Cunningham, Clark E., 94(annot)

Damrong Rajanubhab, Prince, 14, 20
Darling, Frank C., 25, 31, 44
Dellinger, D., 116(annot)
Devakul, Tanaumsri, 138
Development Assistance Committee, 45
de Young, John E., 92
Dhani Nivat (Daninivat, Bidyalabh Bridhyakorn), 14, 15
Dibble, Charles R., 115
Direck, Khun, 7(annot)
Diskul, Subhadradis, 109(annot)
Dobby, E. H. G., 4
Döhring, Karl Siegfried, 5
Dotson, Lillian Ota, 125
Drans, Jean, 20
DuBois, Cora, 5
Dulayachinda, Medhi, 30
Duriyanga, Phra Chen, 113

Economic Commission for Asia and the Far East (ECAFE), 9, 80, 123, 135

Elsbree, Willard H., 45
Embree, John F., 5, 93, 125
Emerson, Rupert, 5
Evers, Hans-Dieter, 25, 50, 93, 94(annot), 104
Exell, F. K., 5

Far Eastern Association of Tropical Medicine, 17
Farzanegan, Farhad, 96
Fifield, Russell H., 5, 9, 45
Finegan, Jack, 105
Fischer, Joseph, 83n, 88
Fisher, Charles Alfred, 5
Fraser, Thomas M., Jr., 36
Freyn, Hubert, 94
Fujiyoshi, Jikai, 132

Gaewchaiyo, Ura, 55
Garcon, Maurice, 13
Geddes, William R., 117(annot)
Gedney, William J., 109, 119(annot)
Gee, Janet G., 122
Gille, Halvor, 120
Ginsburg, Norton, 6
Girling, J. C. S., 34
Goley, Frank, 6
Goldsen, Rose K., 94
Gorden, W. M., 61, 70
Gordon, Bernard K., 6, 45
Goshal, Kumar, 34
Government House Printing Office, Thailand, 118
Graham, Henry, 94
Graham, Juanita, 94
Graham, Walter A., 6
Griswold, Alexander B., 15, 16(annot), 109, 109(annot)
Guskin, Alan E., 84

Haas, Mary R., 109, 110
Hall, D. G. E., 7, 21(annot)
Halpern, A. M., 45
Hampe, Rudolph W. E., 107(annot)
Hanks, J. R., 115
Hanks, Lucien M., 74, 94, 95, 115
Hanna, Willard A., 36
Hansakul, Chakra, 55
Haring, Joseph E., 74
Harrison, Brian, 7
Harvard University, 124
Hatch, Raymond N., 88
Hauck, Hazel M., 95

Hay, Stephen N., 125
Hayden, Howard, 85(annot)
Heine-Geldern, Robert, 7
Hickey, Gerald C., 117
Hindley, Donald, 26
Hinton, Peter, 115
Hirschman, Albert O., 74
Hoath, James R., 36
Hobbs, Cecil, 126
Horrigan, Frederick James, 36, 37
Huff, Lee W., 26, 32, 117(annot)
Hughes, Rufus B., 62
Hunter, Guy, 85(annot), 116
Huntrakoon, Yune, 75(annot)
Hutchinson, W. E., 21(annot)
Huvanandana, Malai, 50

Ibrahim, A. Rashid, 50
Ichikawa, Kenjiro, 126
Iijima, Shigeru, 132
Indiana University, 87
Ingersoll, Jasper, 66, 105, 107
Ingram, James C., 62, 70
Inoki, Masamichi, 46
Insor, D., 7
Institute of Southeast Asian Studies, 136
International Association of Universities, 85
International Bank for Reconstruction and Development, 77
International Political Science Association, 126(annot)
International Translations, 78
Inthachat, Vichien, 70
Isaraphundh, Glom, 62
Ishii, Yoneo, 105
Iwata, Keiji, 132

Jacob, Judith M., 128
Jacobs, Milton, 96
Janlekha, Kamol Odd, 62
Janowitz, Morris, 34
Jittemana, Phimal, 62
Joint Thai-U.S. Military Research and Development Center, 35, 123
Jotikasthere, Sasinee, 129
Jotikasthira, Ampar, 88
Judd, Laurence C., 37, 63, 116(annot)

Kanchanadul, Veeravat, 128
Kandre, Peter, 117(annot)
Kaochareon, Rapee, 20

Karnjanaprakorn, Choop, 37, 97
Kaufman, Howard K., 37, 97
Keesing, Donald B., 63
Kennedy, J., 7
Keyes, Charles F., 26, 38, 97, 119(annot)
Keyfitz, Nathan, 38
Kickert, Robert W., 32, 115(annot), 137
King, John A., 74
Kingsbury, Robert C., 8
Kingshill, Konrad, 38, 116(annot)
Kirsch, A. Thomas, 94(annot), 106, 119(annot)
Klausner, William, 98, 106, 110
Koll, Michael G., Jr., 122
Kongset, Surang, 129
Konoshima, Sumiya, 127
Kozicki, Richard, 127
Krisanamis, Phairach, 63
Kuhn, Isabel, 116
Kunstradter, P., 115(annot), 116, 117(annot), 117

Lack, Donald F., 8
Lam-Toai, 90
Landon, Kenneth Perry, 15, 16, 106, 117
la Loubère, Simon de, 15
Larkin, John A., 2
Lavangkura, Yen, 106
Lebar, Frank M., 117
Lee, S. Y., 63
Leidecker, Kurt F., 107(annot)
le May, Reginald S., 16, 98, 110, 111
Lingat, Robert, 31
Litchfield, Whiting, Boune & Associates, 39
Loftus, John A., 63
Lomax, Louis E., 46
Long, Millard F., 64, 68, 119(annot)
Low, Major James, 20(annot)
Luykx, Nicolaas G. M., 39
Lyman, Albert, 32

MacDonald, Alexander, 8
Madge, Charles, 39
Maitri, Kalyan, 22(annot)
Manndorff, Hans, 117(annot)
Marlowe, D., 116(annot)
Marlowe, G., 116(annot)
Marsh, Harry W., 55
Martin, James V., Jr., 21, 46

Martins, R. F., 16(annot)
Mason, John Brown, 127
Matthews, Noel, 130
Maxwell, William E., 98
Maynard, Paul, 40
McCusker, Henry F., 120
McFarland, Bertha Blount, 21
McGee, T. G., 39
McLane, Charles B., 46
McVey, Ruth T., 128
Meagher, Robert F., 75
Meksawan, Arsa, 40
Miles, D. J., 115(annot)
Mills, Lennox A., 8
Ministry of Agriculture, 79, 80
Ministry of Commerce and Communications, 17
Ministry of Economic Affairs, 81
Ministry of Education, 87
Ministry of Finance, 32
Ministry of the Interior, 118
Ministry of National Development, 81
Mitani, Katsumi, 75
Mizuno, Koichi, 132
Modelski, George, 34
Moerman, Michael, 64, 94(annot), 99, 117(annot)
Moffat, Abbot Low, 16
Mokarapong, Thawatt, 26
Montgomery, John D., 46
Moore, Daniel E., 27
Morgan, Theodore, 75
Mosel, James N., 51, 99, 111
Mote, F. W., 117(annot)
Motooka, Takeshi, 64, 133
Mousny, André, 64
Mozingo, David, 47
Mueller, F. Max, 111
Mulder, J. A. Niels, 94(annot), 100
Murray, Charles, 40
Muscat, Robert J., 75, 76
Musgrave, John K., 117
Myint, Hla, 65, 85
Myrdal, Gunnar, 65

Nairn, Ronald C., 88
National Culture Institute, 112
National Economic Development Board of Thailand, 44, 76, 78, 81
National Institute of Development Administration of Thailand, 135
National Research Council of Thailand, 121, 127, 136

National Statistic Office of Thailand, 79, 80, 81, 129
Neher, Clark D., 40, 51
Neuchterlein, Donald E., 27, 47
Nims, Cyrus R., 41
Noranitipandungkarn, Chakrit, 41
Noss, Richard, 85(annot)
Nunn, G. Raymond, 128

O'Hara, Michael N., 122(annot)

Paauw, Douglas S., 65
Pallegoix, Jean Baptiste, 16
Pandit, Shrikrishna A., 59
Panitpakdi, Prot, 65
Parish, H. Carroll, 127
Parker, Glen L., 76
Pattiya, Akom, 41
Pendleton, Robert L., 8
Perlo, Victor, 34
Peterson, Alex, 47
Pfanner, David E., 107
Pfanner, M. Ruth, 6
Phillips, Herbert P., 27, 30, 94(annot), 95, 100
Phowaathii, Dharmmakhaam, 41
Pickerell, Albert, 27
Piker, Steven, 94(annot), 100, 101, 107
Platenius, Hans, 66
Poole, Peter A., 117
Poowanatnuruk, Prakarn, 41
Porter, Willis P., 86
Pramuanwidhya, Udom, 13(annot)
Prime Minister of Thailand, Office of, 10
Prinyayogavipulya, 107
Promoj, Seni, 16
Public Administration Service, 52, 57
Punyodyana, Boonsanong, 94(annot)
Purachatra, Prem, 112
Purcell, Victor, 118
Pye, Lucien W., 27

Rabibhadana, Akin, 17
Raksasataya, Amara, 128
Ralis, Max, 94
Ramakomud, Sriprinya, 70
Reeve, W. D., 52
Rekaruchi, Salao, 13(annot)
Research Publications, Publishers in the Microfilms, 136
Richter, H. V., 70
Riggs, Fred W., 28, 31, 52

Index

Rogers, Everett, 89
Roop, D. H., 116(annot)
Rothman, Kenneth I., 83n
Royal Siamese Government, 22
Royal Thai Government Gazette, 138
Rozental, Alek A., 66
Rubenstein, Alvin Z., 123
Ruenyote, Suwan, 115(annot)
Russell, Avery, 138
Ryan, John William, 42

Sagara, Iichi, 133
Saihoo, Patya, 118
Sarasas Bholakarn, 17
Sato, Koji, 133
Satorn, Pinyo, 89
Saund, Dalip, 101
Sayre, Francis Bowes, 21, 22(annot)
Schaaf, C. Hart, 9
Schecter, Jerrold, 108
Schuler, Edgar, 86
Schweisguth, P., 112
Seidenfaden, Erik, 21(annot), 101
Semthiti, Theb, 52
Shaplen, Robert, 9
Sharp, Lauriston, 28, 101, 102, 115
Sharto, H. L., 128
Shaw, Archibald B., 86
Shimaoka, Helene R., 129
Shor, Edgar L., 53
Siam Directory, 139
Siam Society, 15, 16, 17, 21, 127, 136
Sibunruang, J. Kasem, 112
Siffin, William J., 50, 53, 55, 56, 77
Silabhundhu, Charoensook, 42
Silcock, T. H., 25, 66, 67, 77, 86, 102
Simmonds, E. H. S., 128
Simmonds, Stuart, 28
Singh, L. P., 28, 47
Sirisumpundh, Kasem, 18
Sithi-Amnuai, Paul, 67, 68
Sitton, Gordon R., 71, 78
Sivaram, M., 28
Siwasariyanon, Witt, 114
Skinner, William G., 118
Smith, Rufus D., 56
Sobhana, Phra Sasana, 107(annot)
Social Science Association Press of Thailand, 107, 137
Sommers, William A., 42, 57
Sookthawee, Tussanee, 84
Soonthornsima, Chinnawoot, 56, 78

Southeast Asia Development Advisory Group (SEADAG), 138
Southeast Asia Treaty Organization (SEATO), 136
Spoelstra, Nyle, 75
Srivisarn Vacha, Phya, 18
Stanton, Edwin F., 34, 47, 48
Starbird, Ann, 129
Steinberg, David Joel, 9
Straits Times Press, 126
Strisavasdi, Boon Chuey, 119
Stucki, Curtis W., 129
Subhanka, Heng R., 110
Sukhum Nayapradit, 56
Suthayakom, Prachak, 128
Sutton, Joseph L., 29
Suvanajata, Titaya, 53
Suwanagul, Kasem, 56

Tambiah, S. J., 102
Tarling, Nicholas, 22
Tennessee Valley Authority, 1
Textor, Robert B., 102
Thailand Information Center, 137
Thamavit, Vibul, 86
Thammasat University, Institute of Public Administration, 50
Thawisomboon, Sanit, 90
The, Lian, xviii(n), 129
Thera, Ven. Nanamoli, 107(annot)
Thisyamondol, Pantum, 68
Thomas, M. Ladd, 29, 54, 119
Thomas, William L., Jr., 5
Thompson, Virginia, 10, 18, 119
Tilman, Robert O., 10, 139
Tulyathorn, Prasit, 29
Tunsiri, Vichai, 29

Udyanin, Kasem, 56, 133
Unakul, Snoh, 71, 73
UNESCO, 85
University of California, 87
Urquhart, W. A. M., 114
U.S. Agency for International Development, 35, 37, 73, 89, 96, 121, 124, 128, 133
U.S. Department of State, Bureau of Intelligence and Research, 125
U.S. Department of Army, Engineer Agency for Resources Inventories, 1
U.S. Information Service (also U.S. Information Agency), 96, 106, 137

Usher, Dan, 68, 71
Utthangkorn, Amphorn, 54

Vajiranana National Library, 21
van der Veur, Paul W., xviii(n), 129
Van Roy, Edward, 69, 103, 119
Vella, Walter F., 4(annot), 18, 22
Vilaichitt, Snit, 54
Von der Mehden, Fred, 10

Wainwright, M. D., 130
Wales, H. G. Quaritch, 10, 11, 18
Walker, A. R., 115(annot)
Warner, Denis, 34
Wells, Kenneth E., 108
Wenk, Klaus, 7, 48
Westphal, Larry E., 74
Wharton, Clifton R., Jr., 78
Wijeyewardene, Gehan, 103
Wilcox, Clair, 79
Wilson, Constance M., 19

Wilson, David A., 29, 30, 34, 35, 119(annot)
Wimoniti, Wira, 57
Wit, Daniel, 32, 48
Wolf, Charles, 48
Wood, W. A. R., 11, 18, 32
Wright, Arnold, 19
Wyatt, David K., 9(annot), 19, 119(annot), 130
Wyss, P., 116(annot)

Yang, Shu-Chin, 69
Yano, Toru, 69, 132
Yassundara, Suparb, 75(annot)
Yatsushiro, Toshio, 43, 54, 108
Young, Gordon, 120
Young, Kenneth T., Jr., 11, 48
Young, Stephen B., 30
Yupho, Dhanit, 113, 114

Zimmerman, Carl C., 69